WHY WE
HIDE

God's plan to free you from

Guilt & Shame

Mark
Brandes

Why We Hide: God's Plan to Free You from Guilt and Shame
Copyright © 2020 by Mark Brandes

ISBN: 978-1-7351-4020-9 (softcover)
ISBN: 978-1-7351-4021-6 (ebook)
ISBN: 978-1-7351402-2-3 (audio)

Library of Congress Cataloging-in-Publication Data
Names: Brandes, Mark. 1953- author.
Title: *Why We Hide: God's Plan to Free You From Guilt And Shame* / Mark Brandes
Identifiers: LCCN 2020910220 ISBN 978-1-7351-4020-9 (tp) ISBN 978-1-7351-4021-6 (ebook)
Subjects: LCSH: Guilt-Religious aspects-Christianity. Shame-Religious aspects-Christianity. Confession. Healing--Religious aspects—Christianity.

Published by Hidden in Him Publishers, Mission Viejo, California, June 2020.
Cover Design: Vanja Dimitrijevic
Illustrations: Mirjana Miljkovic
Interior Design: Doug Williams

To April,

Thank you for loving me
through all of my hiding.

Love you always, B

CONTENTS

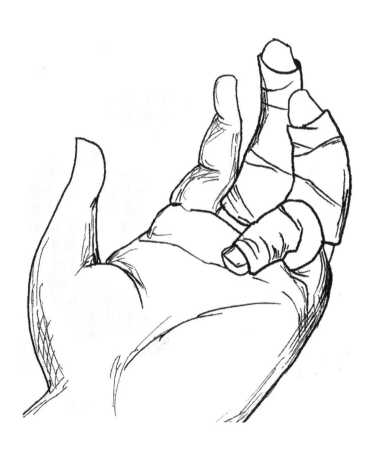

INTRODUCTION

*Therefore, if anyone cleanses himself from what is dishonorable, he will
be a vessel for honorable use, set apart as holy, useful to the master of the
house, ready for every good work.*

2 Timothy 2:21

Yᴏᴜ'ʀᴇ ʜɪᴅɪɴɢ sᴏᴍᴇᴛʜɪɴɢ. You know it. I know it. And of
course, God knows it.

You don't have to do this. What you're covering up has you in the
grip of guilt, shame, and fear. I know it's painful, but *there is a way
out*. In His love, God provided a way, but you have to trust Him.
This will require changes in how you think and how you live, but
you can find freedom.

I know because I hide as well. I spent decades hiding in darkness
before I found freedom in the place God provides…His refuge. God
awakened me out of my secret life one Sunday afternoon:

Blood streamed down my forearm and onto the shiny white floor
as I ran through the emergency room doors. The wad of paper towels

I grabbed just before I drove myself the four miles to the hospital wasn't enough to stem the flow from my left-hand fingers.

"I just cut my hand, and I need some help," I said to the receptionist, who looked first at me, and then down at the scarlet red trail I had left behind.

She waved at a chair and said, "You better sit down and take it easy. What did you do to yourself?"

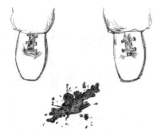

"I ran my fingers through a table saw about 10 minutes ago."

"Let me take a look. Did you cut off your whole finger?"

"No, not the whole finger, but the top of my middle finger just got vaporized. I didn't have anything to pick up."

I felt so stupid. I'm sure in junior high wood shop, the teacher spent at least one entire class on table saw safety. I probably spent that class daydreaming about Leina, Carol, or some other junior high crush when I should have been taking notes about not putting my hand on the other side of the saw blade while it's moving at 7000 rpm.

"Wow," the receptionist said, "you kinda messed yourself up there."

"Yeah, I got carried away trimming my fingernails."

My feeble attempt at humor broke the tension, as I joined the reception nurse in examining my fingers. My middle finger had gotten the worst of the accident. The entire pad under my fingernail had disappeared, and I saw bits of white bone peeking out through all the raw flesh. My ring finger and little finger also had their issues, but they survived, for the most part.

As I lay back on the examining table, waiting for the doctor, I had a chance to reflect on the accident. The moment after I ran my fingers through that saw, I realized I had done much more damage than a Band Aid would fix. I remember thinking: *I'm surprised I haven't done something like this before. I've worked with power equipment for years, screwed down the roof of a 50-foot-tall metal barn with no safety line! Considering all the risky stuff I've done in my life, I've been pretty lucky.*

To be honest, I'm not lucky. I've been protected by God for so many years, but today felt different. I believe God intended this as a wake-up call. He wanted my attention about concealing some major wrongdoings in my life, and He used a table saw to get it. Effective method of correction, don't you think?

I BELIEVE GOD INTENDED THIS AS A WAKE-UP CALL. HE WANTED MY ATTENTION ABOUT CONCEALING SOME MAJOR WRONGDOINGS IN MY LIFE

That day changed *everything* for me. But I'm getting ahead of myself. Let me back up so you know why I might say this. It won't take too long, and you'll get the full picture.

SNEAKY TWERP

As a kid, I did things I knew I shouldn't…I was a sneaky twerp, I'd say. When it came to discipline and teaching character, my dad lacked the patience to weather those storms. He took the easy way out. He'd spank me until I'd cry and then felt he had taken care of his responsibility.

My dad served as a pastor of a Christian church. I think he and my mom assumed I had a strong moral compass because I went to church with them. Nope. Not so much. My compass just *pointed toward me*, toward what my appetites dictated. My universe surrounded me, and my parents didn't discourage that attitude.

Training up a child in godly character and discipline requires more than just a few swats on the backside. *A teacher/student relationship involving open, honest dialogue causes wisdom to move from adult to child.* I'm not blaming my dad; I'm not a victim here. I've had plenty of years to straighten these patterns out myself.

COLLEGE DAZE

When I left home at 18, I began a lifestyle that would cost me dearly. I started drinking as a freshman in college—a cute little Christian college, I might add. I hung around with a bunch of upperclassmen and got swept up into their weekend parties. Miller's Malt Liquor was my DOC (Drug of Choice). Hosting my own drunken blowouts soon

followed. I became a walking illustration of a *hedonist*, treating the pursuit of pleasure as the most important thing in life. Comfort and self-gratification became my idols.

In college, I lived as a bigger version of the same kid who would sneak around his mom's kitchen looking for the hidden cookies. I enjoyed a distorted satisfaction in the pursuit of my self-focused life, but I despised the guilt and shame of my self-gratification, and my lack of integrity. Now, when I look back at those times, I shake my head in sorrow.

Do you look back on your life and wish for something different? I do. I wish I would have had more accountability. No one challenged my lifestyle. No one asked me if I thought my life honored God while I claimed to be a Christian. No one invited me into confession. No one handed me a book like this that drilled down to my core weaknesses.

In his book *You Can Change*, author Tim Chester sums up exactly what I needed: "I need people who regularly ask me about my walk with God, readily challenge my behavior, and know about my temptations. I need my friend Samuel, who often asks, "What's the question you don't want me to ask you?"[1]

THE SIN MANAGER

If a box existed holding all of my sin issues, the label on that messy space might read: "Lack of Self-Discipline." Peeking inside the box, you would see a lack of self-control with my "comfort idols": food, alcohol, money, and sex. For years, I ignored and hid these "pockets of sin" from other people, and at the same time I also ignored the promptings of God to change.

I buried my offenses pretty well. If you and I got together for a chat over coffee, you would walk away from our time together believing I controlled everything in my life. You would be wrong. You would have experienced a conversation with a skilled "sin manager."

You know, sin habits have a way of getting more serious and more deadly when they go unchecked. Some days, I would have my private happy hour while driving home with a 25-ounce Foster's

YOU KNOW, SIN HABITS HAVE A WAY OF GETTING MORE SERIOUS AND MORE DEADLY WHEN THEY GO UNCHECKED.

Ale in my hand. I had become good at coddling and caressing my lack of self-control in drinking…up until the day I almost cut off three fingers. By the way, if you're wondering, I hadn't been drinking the day I had the "accident" with the saw.

ENSLAVED

A verse written by the Apostle Peter summed up my life: "Whatever overcomes a person, to that he is enslaved" (2 Peter 2:19b).

Enslaved. What a sad scene. A grown up "boy man" who worshipped comfort idols in his own little cell. Those worship services focused on me…my desires…what made me feel good right now (and Satan's whispers of shame would make me feel like dirt later).

In hindsight, the Holy Spirit worked to reveal how comfortable I had become in keeping my faults covered. He would whisper in my ear how my lack of self-control and my drinking stood in the way of a closer walk with God. My habitual sin caused me to not pursue God's plan for the good works He wanted for me. I began using spiritual earplugs…ignoring those whispers for me to change.

IN HINDSIGHT, THE HOLY SPIRIT WORKED TO REVEAL HOW COMFORTABLE I HAD BECOME IN KEEPING MY FAULTS COVERED.

(By the way, I don't hear whispers in my ears from Satan or from the Holy Spirit. I thought it might be comforting for you to know that. Throughout the book, when I talk about "whispers" I'm just referring to thoughts any of us might have that stem from good or bad sources).

MERCY AND HOPE

Back in the emergency room, as I looked at my hand which still had five fingers attached (though one seemed a bit shorter now), I became aware of how merciful God had been through this whole accident. This could have been a lot worse. Typing this sentence would be much more difficult if I didn't have all three of those fingers.

> He [God] disciplines us for our good, that we may share his holiness. For the moment all discipline seems painful rather than pleasant, but later it yields the peaceful fruit of righteousness to those who have been trained by it (Hebrews 12:10b-11).

> God's discipline can be abrupt and painful, but worth it. "Don't you see how wonderfully kind, tolerant, and patient God is with you? Does this mean nothing to you? Can't you see that his kindness is intended to turn you from your sin?" (Romans 2:4 NLT).

God kindly allowed me to keep my fingers. That fact brought me to my knees and to a place of repentance over my rebelliousness in drinking.

> "Therefore, I urge you, brothers and sisters, in view of God's mercy, to offer your bodies as a living sacrifice, holy and pleasing to God — this is your true and proper worship" (Romans 12:1 NIV).

If only I had practiced worship that way.

A Vow...Better Late Than Never

In the week following the accident, the word "vow" kept coming up in my thoughts. The time had arrived to make a vow, and so I did. I vowed to not drink again. Finished, for the rest of my life. Next to choosing to follow Jesus, and asking my wife, April, to marry me, this was the most important decision I've made.

The concept of this book, *Why We Hide*, hadn't occurred to me before that day, but in hindsight, God lovingly yet effectively ripped  a hole in my hiding place. His light had broken through into my dark space. Together, God and I burned down the saloon in my heart. The vow I took was long overdue.

In so many ways, the torching of my saloon began a new life for me. Because of that decision, my "elephant sin" of undisciplined drinking no longer stands in the way of the good works God has planned for me while I'm still here on Earth.

Hindsight is so valuable. Looking back over the past 20 years, I can see how ignoring the conviction of the Holy Spirit caused me to miss out on so many of the good works God had planned for me. I trust God will redeem my remaining years and allow me the opportunity to share a few truths He has revealed.

The testimony of a transformed heart, desiring to be like Christ, should be shared with others. God receives glory when hearts grow in godliness. His glory must be the end game.

GOD PROVIDES A WAY TO REMOVE THE HIDING PLACE FROM OUR LIVES, BUT WE HAVE TO TRUST IN GOD'S LOVE FOR US WHEN WE DISOBEY.

Your issue may not be drinking, but there's something hiding in your life. *Only you know what you're keeping secret, and only you know how uncomfortable that makes you. Whatever it is you're working hard to cover up, there's hope for freedom from hiding.*

THE BEST NEWS

Good news exists here. God provides a way to remove the hiding place from our lives, but we have to trust in God's love for us when we disobey. Our hope lies here. To find freedom, we need to partner with Him in tearing down the walls we have taken years to build. If you're someone who has been covering up because of fear and shame, there's hope you can break out of your self-imposed prison and experience the freedom God has for you.

I'd like to introduce you to the God you may not have met yet… the loving God who desires to walk closely with you. Your attempt to conceal your wrongs from a trustworthy God because of fear is unnecessary, and that's what *Why We Hide* is all about. God wants to restore us to a whole relationship with Him, and He also wants our relationships in this world to be healthy. These changes won't happen overnight, but you have my word, they can happen.

WAKE-UP CALL

I don't want you running your hand through a table saw. There's no fun in it. But you need a wake-up call. You know it's true. Whatever you are hiding calls out of the darkness to be revealed, to find some daylight. You might be pushing away thoughts like this, but somewhere in the back of your mind, you want freedom. I kept my sin of undisciplined drinking a secret for over 40 years until I made the decision to pursue release from the prison of my self-induced guilt and shame.

Hopefully this book will be your wake-up call. I can only pray God uses it in your life as He used a 7000-rpm saw blade in mine.

FINDING FREEDOM

We all need to partner with God in finding freedom. *Why We Hide* will guide you through a process of coming out of your hiding place and drawing close to God, no longer living in fear, guilt, and shame, but enjoying the love, intimacy, joy, and celebration of freedom with Jesus. Let's venture out on the path together. You've got nothing to lose, and lots to gain. Great news lies ahead.

Throughout *Why We Hide*, I'm going to remind you of this: *You're not alone. Everyone has a hiding place.*

FOR DISCUSSION

1. This chapter opens with the verse from 2 Timothy 2:21. This verse refers to cleansing oneself from "dishonorable things" so one might be useful to Christ in His Kingdom. Share how this has or has not been a priority for you.

_____

_____

_____

_____

_____

_____

2. Romans 2:4 says God's kindness and patience lead us to repentance. Share your observations about how this has been true in your life.

_____

_____

_____

_____

_____

_____

3. In 2 Peter 2:19, the Apostle Peter writes that people are enslaved by things that "overcome" them. If you are comfortable doing so, share about something you feel overcome by.

_____

_____

_____

_____

_____

_____

CHAPTER 1

GRACE AND MERCY

"I am a God who is near," says the LORD. *"I am also a God who is far away. No one can hide where I cannot see him," says the* LORD. *"I fill all of heaven and earth," says the* LORD.

Jeremiah 23:23-24 NCV

FIREWORKS AND TESTOSTERONE. Nothing could go wrong with that combination, right? Why do boys (or men for that matter) often enjoy blowing up things? I'm no exception. When I got together with my cousins, Alfred and Charlie Sammann, on their family's farm outside of Dimmitt, Texas, we found a lot of fun in watching something explode.

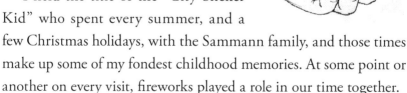

I held the title of the "City Slicker Kid" who spent every summer, and a few Christmas holidays, with the Sammann family, and those times make up some of my fondest childhood memories. At some point or another on every visit, fireworks played a role in our time together.

One summer, I brought along a surprise for my cousins. I had visited Mexico and brought back a bunch of M-80s. Rumor had it these babies exploded with the equivalent power of an eighth of a stick of dynamite. I've since learned that rumor is not true, but I have to say, the blast of an M-80 ramped up our appreciation of powerful fireworks. We heard M-80s were a plastic explosive (also not true), and they exploded in water (True!!!). Of course, we had to give it a shot.

DON'T TRY THIS AT HOME

My uncle had a pond in front of his house which served as a fishing hole and swimming pond. Uncle Ernest stocked it with rainbow trout, which he had flown in from Colorado. What better place to experiment with our firepower than Uncle Ernest's pond, we thought! What could it hurt?

We waited until sunset. My cousins and a couple of their friends gathered around to see what would happen. I lit up the first M-80 and tossed it into the middle of the pond. A moment later, after the M-80 sank below the surface, pyrotechnic ecstasy happened for five teenage boys as the entire pond lit up in a flash. I remember a geyser about 3 feet high shooting out of the water, and then huge ripples radiating in all directions from the center of the pond. One explosion seemed to require more, and so each of us followed up with our own deafening contribution.

By the decibel level of our yelping and hollering you would've thought our favorite football team had just won a bowl game. What a rush…until Uncle Ernest's prize trout began floating to the surface of the pond!

RIPPLES OF DEATH

In our excitement over the fireworks, we created ripples of death. I don't remember how many fish died; I just remember the flashes, the explosions, and the geysers…and then one ticked-off uncle.

Thousands of years ago, ripples of death affected all of us. Some of you might not believe the truth of God's Creation of the first humans, but their story in Genesis explains so much of why our lives seem off the rails today.

A Story from Long Ago

As a young kid, I remember learning about Adam and Eve in Sunday School at my dad's church:

> So God created man in his own image, in the image of God he created him; male and female he created them. And God blessed them.
>
> The LORD God took the man and put him in the garden of Eden to work it and keep it. And the LORD God commanded the man, saying, "You may surely eat of every tree of the garden, but of the tree of the knowledge of good and evil you shall not eat, for in the day that you eat of it you shall surely die" (Genesis 1:27-28b,; 2:15-17).

God created Adam and Eve, made a wonderful garden for them to live in, gave them a purpose of tending His creation, and only asked them to follow one command. He told them not to eat the fruit of one special tree, the Tree of the Knowledge of Good and Evil. At the same time, God gave Adam and Eve the free will to make choices. Adam and Eve possessed the ability to obey Him, but God allowed His creations the freedom to disobey as well.

GOD CREATED ADAM AND EVE, MADE A WONDERFUL GARDEN FOR THEM TO LIVE IN, GAVE THEM A PURPOSE OF TENDING HIS CREATION, AND ONLY ASKED THEM TO FOLLOW ONE COMMAND.

THE INTIMACY OF A WALK WITH GOD

In the Garden of Eden, God, the Creator of the Universe, walked alongside these human beings. God brought Himself down to their level, so He could have an intimate relationship with them. God's presence and His love provided a blessing for these humans which they enjoyed daily.

We see this happen over and over again throughout the history of God's relationship with His people. The theme winds its way through the Bible, and it culminates with Christ's birth, His sharing of the Good News of the gospel, His death and resurrection, and the gift of the Holy Spirit to be our Comforter and our Counselor.

NOT ASHAMED

Genesis 2:25 tells us: "…the man and his wife were both naked and were not ashamed."

Adam and Eve's nakedness was symbolic of their innocence, and spoke volumes about transparency, vulnerability, and intimacy. God intends this for our relationship with Him, too.

When God placed a naked Adam and Eve in the Garden of Eden, there was no sin, no guilt, and no shame. The garden was the only perfect place…at least for a time. The close, intertwined relationship between God and Man could be illustrated like this:

In their nakedness, Adam and Eve had nothing to keep secret from each other, and nothing existed to hide from God. Unfortunately, for Adam and Eve (and for the rest of us), the original intimacy between God and His created children didn't last long.

WE HAVE A VISITOR, HONEY

Word to the wise…if you run across a talking snake, turn around and walk away. Don't engage, okay? Don't chit-chat. And stop smoking whatever you've been smoking.

Eve would have been wise to turn around and run:

> Now the serpent was more crafty than any other beast of the field that the LORD God had made. He said to the woman, "Did God actually say, 'You shall not eat of any tree in the garden'?" And the woman said to the serpent, "We may eat of the fruit of the trees in the garden, but God said, 'You shall not eat of the fruit of the tree that is in the midst of the garden, neither shall you touch it, lest you die.'" But the serpent said to the woman, "You will not surely die. For God knows that when you eat of it your eyes will be opened, and you will be like God, knowing good and evil" (Genesis 3:1-5).

The enemy of God and man appears in the Garden when Satan disguises himself as a beautiful snake. Apparently, he didn't seem disgusting to Eve, and Ezekiel 28:13 says he looked like a piece of jewelry.

BLURRING THE LINES

Before Satan showed up, Adam and Eve had been walking closely with God and obeying His commands. Their lives said: *I Worship*

God. They showed humility before God by their obedience, at least for a time.

Every day, we're faced with this decision: *Do we obey God? Or do we reconsider His commands in light of our desires?* Satan proposes an option to Eve. He suggests Eve think differently about God and the path He required. Author Dietrich Bonhoeffer writes: "The command (from God), suggests the Serpent, needs to be explained and interpreted. Man must decide for himself what is good by using his conscience and his knowledge of good and evil…Doubt and reflection take the place of spontaneous obedience."[2] When God gives commands, He doesn't intend for us to weigh those commands, deciding how we feel about obeying.

WHEN GOD GIVES COMMANDS, HE DOESN'T INTEND FOR US TO WEIGH THOSE COMMANDS, DECIDING HOW WE FEEL ABOUT OBEYING.

Satan appeals to the pride of Eve. He deceives her by implying God has withheld something she needs. In doing so, Satan undermines her trust in God. Satan plants the thought into Eve's mind she should be equal to God. When Eve considers Satan's temptation, she begins to doubt God's goodness, and she starts to covet the fruit God told her she cannot have. Satan succeeded in deceiving Eve.

Pride works through comparison. We evaluate our circumstances, and our pride will tell us we need something more, or something different. By thinking that way, we show our lack of trust in God to supply our needs. *Satan specializes in planting seeds of doubt and mistrust.*

Pride pushes us to say, "I Worship Me" instead of "I Worship God." This is the pattern of life Satan loves. Satan wants a worship distortion in every human's life. His greatest desire is to have more and more people live in the I Worship Me space.

SATAN'S LIE

How did Satan deceive Eve? The same way he does with you and me: a little truth and a huge lie. He told Eve this lie: *"You will not surely die."* Then he told the truth: *"If you eat of the Tree of Knowledge you will know good and evil."* Satan didn't tell Eve this truth: Knowing good and evil can be harmful in so many ways.

Today, Satan does the same with us: he tempts us with some sweet looking morsel of bait wrapped around a big and painful hook.

THE FALL

Check out what happens next:

> So when the woman saw that the tree was good for food, and that it was a delight to the eyes, and that the tree was to be desired to make one wise, she took of its fruit and ate, and she also gave some to her husband who was with her, and he ate (Genesis 3:6).

Elyse Fitzpatrick writes about Eve's fateful choice:

Why did Eve choose to disobey God? Look again at three words in the verse: *good, delight, desirable.* These are words that illustrate the motivation behind actions…The truth about our choices is that we always choose what we believe to be our best good. We always choose what we believe will bring us the most delight.[3]

Eve was deceived, but then, to make matters worse, Adam also ate the fruit. Instead of falling for Satan's deception, Adam knowingly rebelled against God by his disobedience. Often, we call what Adam and Eve did "The Fall." This falling away of Adam and Eve from God occurred not only because of Eve's deception, but because of Adam's disobedience.

Disobedience and the first human's self-determination sent the world into a tailspin. Because of  Adam and Eve's wrongdoing, every descendant of this couple will be born with a predisposition to live in the I Worship Me place. Why should we be surprised the word "Mine" comes out of the mouth of a toddler so early in life?

SHAME AND DEATH COME INTO THE GARDEN

Adam and Eve got more than they bargained for when they disobeyed God. They became more enlightened about the reality of good and evil: "Then the eyes of both were opened, and they knew that they were naked. And they sewed fig leaves together and made themselves loincloths" (Genesis 3:7).

Something huge just happened…an explosive rippling in the cosmos that didn't make a sound. *Adam and Eve's eyes opened up to evil, and for the first time, they felt shame.* Disobedience of God caused guilt, shame, and fear to enter God's perfect Creation. The first human's poor choice to eat forbidden fruit caused a permanent gap between God and His creation, and everything God created began to die.

Two disobedient bites of fruit in the Garden. That's all it took to cause ripples of death through all of history.

THE HIDING BEGINS

Satan loves this. Because Adam and Eve made the choice to worship their desires rather than God's, we see relationships broken. Adam and Eve no longer live in freedom and intimacy with God. After the Fall, they see their nakedness as wrong and shameful, and they no longer walk closely in the Garden with their Creator/Father. They begin to hide.

> And they heard the sound of the LORD God walking in the garden in the cool of the day, and the man and his wife hid themselves from the presence of the LORD God among the trees of the garden. But the LORD God called to the man and said to him, "Where are you?" And he said, "I heard the sound of you in the garden, and I was afraid, because I was naked, and I hid myself" (Genesis 3:8-10).

In a moment, the intimacy God created disappears. Adam and Eve begin to cover up, revealing less of themselves, and they hide from God. When we pridefully place our desires above God, we bear this consequence: the price of making the I Worship Me choice. Sin causes separation, and guilt and shame cause confusion. To illustrate the new relationship between God and Man, it looks like this:

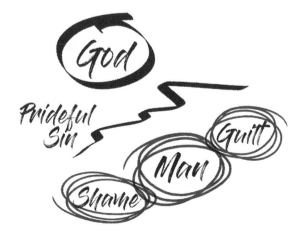

The Separation

Disobedience has consequences. When Adam and Eve experienced the guilt and the shame of their wrongs, they wanted to hide, because *they didn't trust God to love them through their brokenness.* A lack of trust made them afraid. We feel the same effects in our lives today.

Before Adam and Eve sinned, God's presence in the Garden did not cause fear, it caused joy. Everything changed because of how they responded to Satan's temptation. In our lives, Satan does the same thing to rob us of joy, power, and intimacy with God. We need to overcome this downward spiral.

After Adam and Eve rebelled against God, He *still* walked in the Garden in the cool of the day. *Their disobedient choices couldn't change God's love for them.* Where does it say God ran into the Garden to scream and shame His kids? But that's what Satan would have you believe. Satan doesn't want us seeking God's forgiveness. He would have us believe we should fear God coming to beat on us. This message contains both a truth and a lie. God pursues us daily, but He wants us to come out of our hiding place so He can show us

Satan doesn't want us seeking God's forgiveness. He would have us believe we should fear God coming to beat on us.

His love, and His protection.

Not only has our unrighteousness separated us from God, but also, when we sin, when we miss the mark, we hide and feel alone. God has given us the power to do something about our aloneness and our desire to cover up. We all need to get to work on pursuing the path out of hiding.

HIDING FROM GOD? REALLY?

After Adam and Eve fell for Satan's deception and temptation, God still called out for His children. He called out in love, not to shame them. "But the LORD God called to the man and said to him, 'Where are you?'" (Genesis 3:9).

Adam and Eve just caused the entirety of God's perfect Creation to begin dying. God doesn't send a lightning bolt down on their heads. He just calls for them. *Wow! Here's a God who shows how He loves His children with patience, love, grace, and mercy.*

May I just take a moment to define a couple of words here? In the context of our relationship with God, "grace" means God gives us what we don't deserve, and "mercy" means God doesn't give us what we do deserve.

JESUS PAID THE ULTIMATE PRICE FOR ADAM AND EVE'S ERRORS, AS WELL AS YOURS AND MINE.

You need to know this God of incredible grace and mercy. Yes, the Bible talks a lot about sin, but here's the deal: We've got to understand the depth of our messed-up lives to appreciate God's loving, merciful plan of redemption.

Adam and Eve's sin didn't surprise God. Before He created them, He already had a plan to cover their wrongs. But this plan required God's Son, Jesus, to die. He laid down His life to satisfy God's anger and wrath because of our wrongs. Jesus paid the ultimate price for Adam and Eve's errors, as well as yours and mine. Christ died to save us from the penalty of living a life of I Worship Me.

BRAINWASHED

We know we have given God a ton of reasons to be angry over our lifetime of brokenness. We feel the emotional ramifications of our actions and assume God has to be pretty ticked off at us.

But we have underestimated how much patience God has, and how much love and forgiveness He has for us. Stories of God's patience and love fill the Bible. God can become righteously angry at times, but He shows so much more mercy and grace than we humans deserve.

Many people have been brainwashed to believe the anger of God focuses on them. Those people don't trust God's faithful love to care for them when they're doing sinful things, just like all of us. Those people believe God holds onto punishment and wrath, waiting to chastise them for all the wrongs they have done.

That's not true of the God we see in the Bible. In His actions toward broken people, God reveals His true character. God reaches out to us, ready to pursue a deeper relationship.

GOD HINTS AT PLAN A

God had every right to destroy Adam and Eve, but God chose mercy.

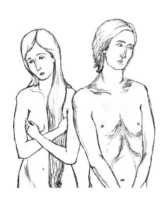

Because of the evil Adam and Eve initiated, God had to make Adam and Eve leave the Garden. If the story of Adam and Eve ended here, it would be pretty depressing for all of us. We would be left shouldering our guilt and our shame with no way back into a relationship with God. Fortunately, the story doesn't end here.

Before God puts Adam and Eve out of the Garden, He does something so loving and so symbolic. *He kneels down from heaven and crafts their clothes.* "And the LORD God made for Adam and for his wife garments of skins and clothed them" (Genesis 3:21).

That one verse says so much about the character of God, and it testifies to His love for us. This act of God paints such a loving picture: The God of the Universe stoops down and becomes a tailor for His disobedient children. He clothes them and covers their nakedness…their brokenness.

Where do you think God got the skins to craft these clothes? He had to kill one of the animals from His perfect Garden. God's Plan A required this, and it's prophetic. God shed blood to cover Adam and Eve's nakedness, and God sent His Son, Jesus Christ, to shed His blood for your sins and mine.

A coincidence? No. God's act of making clothes for Adam and Eve is just the beginning of His redemption plan. "Indeed, under the law almost everything is purified with blood, and without the shedding of blood there is no forgiveness of sins" (Hebrews 9:22).

God's redemptive story for us begins when He covers Adam and Eve by sacrificing an animal, and this points to how He covers your faults and mine. God shows His grace and mercy at work right here. When God covered Adam and Eve, He illustrated what the coming Messiah would do — shed His blood to cover the price for our guilt and shame.

Don't miss the significance of what just happened. God's children had no power to deal with their disobedience, their nakedness, and so God did it for them. He has done the same for us as well. God covers our broken lives through the sacrifice of His Son, Jesus Christ.

A God who becomes a tailor for pride-filled, self-determined kids. You gotta love that.

God's Plan to Free You from Guilt and Shame

God wants to restore us to the intimacy of the Garden, and He offers redemption and renewal to us every day. He wants His children (you and me) to feel this closeness. God's plan to deal with our sin for eternity shows His commitment to restoring the relationship He once had with Adam and Eve in the Garden. God looks forward to intimacy with all of us. Because of God's plan, one day, we will once more enjoy this kind of relationship with Him in Heaven.

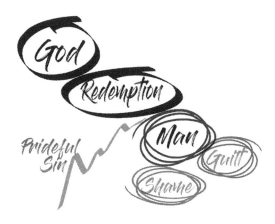

A long time after Adam and Eve died, God revealed His plan for redemption through Jesus.

This redemption created a bridge between God and His Creation, and forever changed the grip of sin, shame and guilt. The couple who brought sin into the world wouldn't know how God would redeem their story, but through Scripture, we know the blessing of the storyline of salvation. Hope for eternity lies only in Jesus Christ. If you're reading this book and your hope lies in yourself or somewhere else than in Christ, you need to read on, because you're mistaken. There is no other hope.

HOW DO WE STOP HIDING?

So now you know the beginnings of why we hide our offenses. The question becomes, how do we leave behind a life of hiding our sin?

God's plan calls us out of our hiding and into His Light. We need to become comfortable shining a whole lot more light on our wrongdoing than we have before. This requires humility. The way out of your hiding begins with some soul searching:

- Where are you disobedient to what God desires of your life?

- What do you think or do that causes you to want to hide?

We're all in this together. We need to offer each other the same love, grace, and mercy God extends to us. Our best chance for leaving our hiding place behind and pursuing the good works God has planned for us begins here. Everyone in the world, including followers of Christ, do I Worship Me things, and we might as well accept the fact we will continually do this. But followers of Christ are people who have had their wrongs covered…covered for eternity.

WE'RE ALL IN THIS TOGETHER. WE NEED TO OFFER EACH OTHER THE SAME LOVE, GRACE, AND MERCY GOD EXTENDS TO US.

Why don't we live in the joy of this truth? We don't live that way because we exist in a culture that doesn't encourage self-revelation or self-examination about wrongdoing. Why? Because our pride doesn't like the resulting feelings of sin, and pride doesn't embrace the cure, which is confession.

I've got bad news for you, and I've got some great news. The bad news is: God knows everything you hide. The great news is the same, but with an addition…*He knows everything you cover up, and He loves you anyway.* God doesn't want you living this way because it causes pain in your life and separation from Him. He wants to wrap His arms around your shoulders, covering your shame with His love. This is where your hope for freedom lies.

God's Plan A is found in Jesus Christ. God covered Adam and Eve's guilt and shame with animal skins that required blood to be shed. His plan to cover our guilt and shame began with sending His Son, Jesus, to shed His blood.

God showed us mercy through His Son's sacrifice because we cannot pay for all of our wrongs. *Because of God's wrath poured out on Jesus, we can have salvation, and eternal life with Him. This is the best news for anyone who is hiding because of sin and shame.*

Remember:

You're not alone. Everyone has a hiding place.

FOR DISCUSSION

1. In Genesis 3:6, Eve saw the forbidden fruit as *good* for food, a *delight* to the eyes, and *desired* to make one wise. Share about an attraction you have to something you think might be forbidden, but you find it to be desirable anyway.

_____

_____

_____

_____

_____

2. Satan asked Eve to *reconsider* God's command about the forbidden fruit in Genesis 3:4-5. Share why you believe we are tempted to reconsider God's commands.

_____

_____

_____

_____

_____

_____

3. After Adam and Eve ate the forbidden fruit, "their eyes were opened" to good and evil, but they immediately wanted to hide. Why do you think that happened?

_____

_____

_____

_____

_____

_____

4. Genesis 3:8-9 tells us that God was calmly walking in the Garden after "the Fall." What does this say about the character of God, and about His desire for a relationship with humans?

_____

_____

_____

_____

_____

_____

5. Hebrews 9:22 reveals that our sins are not forgiven without blood being shed. Why do you think this is true? What does this say about God's view of sin?

_____

_____

_____

_____

_____

_____

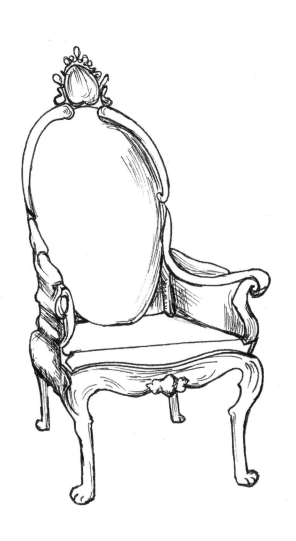

CHAPTER 2

DISTORTED WORSHIP

Pride is the mother hen under which all other sins are hatched.

C.S. Lewis

1. There is a God.
2. You ain't Him.

Dan Phillips

THE DINNER HOUR brought pain for 6-year-old Katherine. By that time of day, her father, well into his usual drunken state, lashed out at the family with constant criticism, and his wife offered little help to protect the children. The home didn't know love.

As far back as second grade, Katherine remembers a craving for connection and attention, and she became skilled at forming close friendships with other girls. Those friendships turned dark in junior high when the peer pressure of Southern California pushed many young girls into habits of anorexia and bulimia. Those junior high friends became Katherine's "skinny posse."

Many days, Katherine would only eat mustard on bread. She found starving herself helped to accentuate her developing figure, which attracted the boys at school. A wonderful, ear-to-ear smile and huge eyes were two of Katherine's most striking features, and they were exaggerated by her anorexic condition.

The difficulty of family life caused Katherine to attempt suicide twice by age 15, surviving both attempts before making a decision to leave home. She bounced through several living situations while working at a local coffee shop to support her $500 monthly rent. At the coffee shop, Katherine met a new friend, Katie, who invited her to join her local church youth group.

Katie knew a couple from the church who recently moved to a large new house with lots of bedrooms, even though their only daughter had just headed off to college. Katie boldly asked the couple if they could consider having Katherine live with them, and they thought it would be a great idea. Katherine met the couple at a Christmas service, and over the winter holiday in 1998, they invited her to live with them in their new home.

A caring, peace-filled life wrapped its arms around Katherine, and she began attending the youth group at her friend's church. With Katie by her side, Katherine found the loving connections she had desired for so many years. In this environment, she came to know Jesus, and His message of love and forgiveness consumed her.

For once in her life, Katherine's "love-tank" seemed to fill. She began making deeper friendships which weren't focused on appearances. For the first time in her life, Katherine had parental figures who cared for her needs and for her future, both spiritually and physically. Soon, Katherine felt a strong desire to be cared for as a daughter.

A teen-age boy took an interest in Katherine, and they began dating. The intimacy of a boy's attention, and his hugs and kisses, drew Katherine closer and closer to a sexual relationship. Knowing this, Katherine's new "foster parents" encouraged the teens to "put the brakes on."

Katherine found herself torn between her all-consuming desire to be loved and obeying the couple who had opened their home to her. Friction developed, and tensions ran high. Katherine began exploring moving in with an aunt who lived on the East Coast. In the summer of 2000, Katherine left Southern California to begin a new life with her aunt in upstate New York.

KATHERINE FOUND HERSELF TORN BETWEEN HER ALL-CONSUMING DESIRE TO BE LOVED AND OBEYING THE COUPLE WHO HAD OPENED THEIR HOME TO HER.

Katherine had no idea the transition would be so hard. Unable to find a church group as she had grown to love in California, Katherine cried almost daily, missing the life she had left. But she did find comfort in the arms of a man, and, at 18, three months after she left California, Katherine became pregnant.

The young man and his family pressured Katherine to "deal with the problem." Broken-hearted and guilt-ridden, she reached out to the couple she had lived with in California. More than anything, Katherine wanted them to jump on a plane, fly to New York, and walk her through her decisions. Katherine recalls the couple merely saying: "We'll pray for you."

My wife, April and I, were that couple who shared our home with Katherine for almost two years, and then turned away when she needed us at a much deeper level. *If April and I had to do it all over, we would be there for Katherine in a heartbeat.*

Katherine chose to have the abortion, knowing God hated her decision. Afterward, in her words, Katherine's life "went black." She wandered far from her faith, feeling rejected both by God as well as His "ambassadors."

Years of self-destructive behaviors involving sex, drugs, and alcohol followed the abortion. Five years after her first pregnancy, Katherine became pregnant again. This time, she had the courage to keep the baby. Her first-born son became her reason to live.

Motherhood didn't fulfill Katherine's craving for love and connection. She still pursued casual relationships which seemed to fill the gaping void in her life, at least for the moment. Five years after the birth of her first child, Katherine became pregnant again and had a second child, this time a daughter.

MOTHERHOOD DIDN'T FULFILL KATHERINE'S CRAVING FOR LOVE AND CONNECTION. SHE STILL PURSUED CASUAL RELATIONSHIPS WHICH SEEMED TO FILL THE GAPING VOID IN HER LIFE...

In 2010, Katherine's only brother James died, just short of his twenty-fifth birthday. His death left Katherine a broken woman, and a deep anger began rising in her heart. This anger caused her to lash out at April with a couple of bitter, vindictive letters, holding her responsible for much of the pain Katherine had experienced. April grieved over the rejection for years.

But a bright spot appeared in Katherine's life. At the encouragement of a friend, she went on a blind date with a man she met online. Eric and his daughter joined Katherine and her two kids for a "play-date," and Katherine fell in love overnight.

One Sunday, Eric and Katherine visited the Free Christian Church in Andover, Massachusetts. Pastor David Midwood had chosen "Prostitutes and Drug Addicts" as his sermon theme, and he embedded in the teaching his testimony of past failures. Eric and

Katherine were stunned at the pastor's confessional transparency, and both said: "If this is what Christianity looks like here, we want in."

I believe the Holy Spirit convicted both Katherine and Eric that day, turning their lives around. Within two weeks, Eric and Katherine were married, and began attending church together. During a study of Jonah, Katherine came to know the true, loving God of second chances. Her heart softened, and she reached out to April, seeking reconciliation.

Not long after, April and I met Katherine at a Starbucks back in California. I had to fight back tears as I watched Katherine and April love on each other in a whole new way. Both women confessed how they had failed each other and shared their joy in this reunion. Great healing occurred that morning in a wonderful God-moment.

THRONES

Everyone worships something. I worshipped my desire for comfort and ease through alcohol. Katherine worshipped the love and care of other people, and given her background, that shouldn't be a surprise. Both Katherine and I came to realize the distortion of our values. We had created idols, and in doing so, we were both living out patterns of distorted worship. In our own way, we both worshipped before altars of our making. Both of our lives said: I Worship Me.

Only one throne exists in a person's life, but we act as if this throne can be shared. Often, followers of Christ might say they have "turned their lives over to Jesus." If we believe this to be true of us, then it would mean Jesus sits on the throne of our lives, right?

If we only lived that way!

Every single day, we make choices which cause us to climb up on the throne of our life. We do that when we rebel against God and we say "I Worship Me." *Our disobedience of God's commands indicates we believe we belong on the throne of our lives, not Jesus. After Adam and Eve's fall, throne climbing became part of our nature.*

God created man with free choice, but free choice can be dangerous because no boundaries exist. Everything is an option. Everything is possible.

THE PRICE OF INTIMACY

Pride lives within a disobedient heart. A prideful heart desires the role of God, to be climbing up on His throne. When options abound, we can be tempted to fall into prideful self-determination, just like Adam and Eve. We make choices serving our desires, not God's.

God created Adam and Eve to have intimacy with Him, but He also wanted their obedience. That's the price of intimacy with God. Instead of obeying God's commandment regarding "the tree of the knowledge of good and evil," they chose instead the path offered to them by Satan. They chose to follow their desires for themselves over God's desires for them.

Satan opposes God, and all God stands for. Yes, he's ticked off he couldn't overthrow all of Heaven so he could sit on God's throne, and now he's attempting to defeat God's children here on Earth.

Satan's no match for the God who created him. For a time, God will allow Satan to exert his power on Earth, but it won't last forever. Trust me, when God finally deals with Satan, it will make all those apocalyptic movie special effects look silly.

THE SIN DISEASE

When Satan brought prideful disobedience to our world, he "infected" everyone with the disease of pride-based behavior, which distorts our worship of God. A self-focused nature, stemming from a heart of pride, lives within us from birth. We all have the disease of prideful sin.

For the purpose of this book, let's define pride like this: *Any thought or action which places one-self or one's desires above or apart from God's commands or directions.* In case you disagree with this definition of pride, let's take a look at some pretty common issues:

TRUST ME, WHEN GOD FINALLY DEALS WITH SATAN, IT WILL MAKE ALL THOSE APOCALYPTIC MOVIE SPECIAL EFFECTS LOOK SILLY.

- **Gossip**…makes YOU feel *better* about YOU.

- **Porn and Lust**…make YOU feel *desired*…make YOU feel *in control.*

- **Abortion**…*relieves* YOU of the evidence and inconvenience of YOUR wrong.

- **Money and Possessions**…make YOU feel *better* about YOU, and *better* than others.

- **Drunkenness and Addictions**…make YOU feel *temporarily comforted.*

- **Gluttony**…makes YOU feel *fulfilled* and *comforted.*

- **Anger and Judgment of Others**…make YOU feel *better* about YOU.

- **Lying**…makes YOU look *better* to others.

By the way: Notice how so many of these pride issues revolve around comparing ourselves to others? Our pride causes us to pursue broken things when we feel as if we don't measure up, and we feel the need for something more. In his book *Mere Christianity*, C.S.Lewis writes: "Pride gets no pleasure out of having something, only out of having more of it than the next man." [4]

I think it's only right to tell you, I am guilty of all of the issues I mentioned above. Yes, every one of them, including abortion. Before my marriage, I dated a young woman who became pregnant with a child I had fathered. In the fear of what others might think, and *only considering the inconvenience of this pregnancy*, we made the decision to abort the child.

I have faced all of the temptations and struggles many of you have faced, and I've fallen down in so many ways. Thankfully, I serve a loving God who helps me up, dusts me off, forgives me, and sends me out with the same words He said to the woman caught in adultery: "Go, and from now on, sin no more"(John 8:11b). Doesn't that sound like a wonderful Father full of grace and mercy?

DENIAL

When you're caught in wrongdoing, what's your go-to response? Would it surprise you if I guessed denial? I do exactly the same.

IF WE FOCUS ON OUR PRIDE THAT'S BEEN HURT, AND OUR SHAME, THEN WE DENY, WE RUN, WE COVER UP.

We deny our faults because our pride is hurt (somehow, we delude ourselves into thinking we have the ability to be perfect). We're ashamed, and we're afraid of judgment.

We *should be led to godly sorrow by our guilt*, but most often, we become ashamed for all the wrong reasons. We feel shame because our pride hurts, and because we feel we look bad in someone else's eyes.

Let's be honest: We should be ashamed because we have offended a Holy God. If we focus on our pride that's been hurt, and our shame, then we deny, we run, we cover up. *We begin to build our hiding place where we can keep our secret sins.*

And Satan wins again. Just like Adam and Eve, he wants us to run and hide from God. The more he can do to push us away from God, the better. But that's not God's desire.

God loves you. He wants you to come out of your hiding place. God wants to be your refuge, your hiding place. He wants an intimate relationship with you. I'm not being inappropriate here, but He wants you to walk through life with Him naked…transparent about the real you.

IDOL WORSHIP

In Cuba, you will find people who follow a religion called "Santeria," a combination of Roman Catholicism and the Yoruba religion from West Africa, similar to voodoo. The people who practice Santeria will often have a small altar in their home where they have a number of symbolic items, and usually a doll, thought to have special powers.

On one of our church's mission trips to Cuba, a friend of mine met a man making these dolls, and he asked whether the man worshipped them as well. The doll maker's response was pretty simple: "No, why would I worship something I made with my own hands?"

Wow, a Cuban idol maker who virtually quotes Scripture: *"Truly, O LORD, the kings of Assyria have laid waste all the nations and their lands, and have cast their gods into the fire. For they were no gods, but the work of men's hands, wood and stone. Therefore they were destroyed"* (Isaiah 37:18-19).

We might chuckle at the wisdom of an idol maker who doesn't bow down to the idols he makes, but we should be so wise. Our brokenness reveals what we value in our lives. We can worship money, sex, food, drugs, alcohol, or more simple things like lying, cheating, or gossip. Those idols might look different from one person to another, but they have one thing in common: they all take our focus off obeying God, and they put our focus on ourselves, and our desires. *Idols cause a worship disorder in our lives.*

WE MIGHT CHUCKLE AT THE WISDOM OF AN IDOL MAKER WHO DOESN'T BOW DOWN TO THE IDOLS HE MAKES, BUT WE SHOULD BE SO WISE.

Paul David Tripp writes: "The deepest issues of the human struggle are not issues of pain and suffering, but the issue of worship, because what rules our hearts will control the way we respond to both suffering and blessing."[5]

When we believe we should be in charge of our pursuits, we live out the same rebellion pattern of Adam and Eve. *We live as if our desires and our pleasures are gods. Every once in a while, we might give some brief consideration to "following God," but for the most part, we live as if our highest priority is our comfort and pleasure. Living that way reveals our worship disorder.*

THE ELEPHANT SIN

Sinful habits begin to grow early in our lives, and they rarely get smaller on their own. What might seem like a minor issue has the ability to grow into a major problem if you don't take care of it quickly. Building a hiding place around your brokenness is like raising a pet elephant inside your home.

Let's suppose you decide you want to raise an elephant as a pet, but you want to keep it a secret from your neighbors. The best idea would be to get an elephant when he's young, right? Baby elephants only weigh 200 pounds when they're born, and they're just 3 feet tall. Sure, you could hide that size elephant.

Maybe you have a friend at the local zoo who sneaks a newborn elephant out of the zoo for you to take home. At night, you back a trailer up to your house and lead your new pet elephant, who you named Tiny, in through the patio door.

You've got the living room all set up as Tiny's bedroom with a bunch of straw on the floor. Little do you know you're committing to provide Tiny with about 300 pounds of food *every* day as he grows to be over 12 feet tall and tips the scales at 10,000 pounds! BTW, at some point, 300 pounds of "processed" food will need to be cleaned up, if you know what I mean.

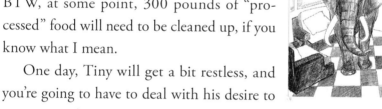

One day, Tiny will get a bit restless, and you're going to have to deal with his desire to roam around. You didn't think about getting Tiny *out* of the house. You just thought about getting Tiny *into* the house.

Like Tiny, the sin that starts small can take over your life. Covering up wrongdoing can become a pattern which encourages more hiding…concealing bigger stuff.

I doubt anyone who begins walking down the road of habitual sin considers how their life will look when their distorted worship begins to control them. I didn't! By the time I considered changing my unrighteous patterns, they were settled in place. My life had become wrapped around those habits, and my relationship with God suffered the effects of those behaviors.

Why? Because I had shoved Jesus over on the throne of my life to make room for my hidden pursuits. Alcohol became an idol for me. Remember: God has every right to be a jealous God because His ways are best. In the life of a follower of Jesus, there will be no other gods. If one appears, God knows how to correct His kids through gracious and loving discipline. As our heavenly Father, God concerns Himself with our character, and He will wake us up to areas we need to change. Table saws get your attention…trust me.

WHAT'S YOUR NICHE?

If you had a key to the door of the place you've created to push away your distorted worship habits, one side of the key will be engraved  with the word "Pride," since all sin originates there. The other side might have another word engraved, which would describe your specific personal weakness. Mine would say "Self-Control." We need to talk about the word that describes your habits.

Don't get defensive now. We've got a long way to go in our conversation about all of this, and if you shut down now and bail out, you'll miss the good stuff. You have to remember, God's not yelling at you. He's just saying, *"Where are you?"* Please, trust God with your weaknesses.

So what's your niche? Have any idea?

If not, I have two exercises for us to do together. But before we start, let's lay this before God and ask for His help. King David wrote a prayer which can help us focus on the messy, ugly stuff of our lives. This prayer should be on our lips daily because it helps clear out our hiding places: "Search me, O God, and know my heart; test me and know my anxious thoughts. Point out anything in me that offends You, and lead me along the path of everlasting life" (Psalm 139:23-24 NLT).

Set this book down, clear your mind as best you can, and start with a prayer of humility. Your pride will want to push away from what we are about to do. Ask the Holy Spirit for a humble heart to ask this question: "What do I think or do that offends my God?"

Now wait. Just sit there for 5-10 minutes and push any thought out of your mind that seems to be unrelated to that question you just asked. Jot down what you sensed the Holy Spirit revealed to you.

Now, let's explore a more emotional side.

Close your eyes and imagine you're in a stadium, surrounded by everyone you've ever met, all the people who have known you since you were born. There's a Jumbotron video screen at the end of the field the size of the one in Cowboy Stadium, 72x160 feet, and a movie of your life begins to roll.

The film shows all the good, the bad, and the ugly of your life. The movie goes super fast until it reaches the ugly stuff, and then it slows to a crawl. All those things you regret having done, said, or thought in your life. The movie reveals everything; nothing's left out, and it's so painful. A hush falls over the stadium because they all know their story will come up soon.

Oh, I forgot to mention. Jesus is standing right next to you, and He has wrapped His arm around your shoulder. He already knows your movie. He's seen it all before.

PAINFUL MOMENTS

What do you see? What's the pattern of your life? What embarrassing, shame-filled moments make you want to run and hide? What scenes would you most like to fast-forward through so no one can see that part of your life? Okay, now stop and do this exercise before we move on, just for a few moments.

Those scenes reveal what you would like to keep secret, and they also show what idol(s) you're worshipping. When you imagine seeing all of your messy life on the screen, and having Jesus's hand on your shoulder, it seems awkward, right? You have difficulty looking at the huge gap between Jesus's holiness and your Jumbotron mess. Jesus

wouldn't be standing next to you with His hand on your shoulder if He didn't love you. Your next step is to trust His love.

As awful as your movie might feel, you should know Jesus doesn't want you to feel shame over your movie. He has intimate knowledge of your broken life because He Himself paid the price God demanded for your wrongs. When soldiers hung Christ on the cross, He dealt with your Jumbotron story.

PRIDE VS. HUMILITY

God *hates* pride, and He also *hates the rebellion it generates*. He hates pride and rebellion because it forced Christ to die on that cross.

> "The fear of the LORD is hatred of evil. Pride and arrogance and the way of evil and perverted speech I hate" (Proverbs 8:13).
>
> "Everyone who is proud in heart is an abomination to the LORD; Assuredly, he will not be unpunished" (Proverbs 16:5 NASB).

God knows pride will draw us away from Him and from our proper posture of a worshipping servant. He knows pride will cause us to disobey His will and this creates a distance from Him. Pride causes all kinds of things to become "gods" in our lives, and we can *make ourselves* the "god" of our life too.

Over 100 times, the Bible mentions the word "pride," or "proud," or my favorite, "haughty," and almost every time, it's in a negative context. There are about 83 mentions of "humble" or "humility," and most are in a positive light.

> The LORD lifts up the humble; he casts the wicked to the ground (Psalm 147:6).
>
> Likewise, you who are younger, be subject to the elders. Clothe yourselves, all of you, with humility toward one another, for "God opposes the proud but gives grace to the humble"(1 Peter 5:5).

Every day we face this battle. Metaphorically, we were born with a prideful DNA strain of I Worship Me. God seeks out those people willing to exchange their prideful living to return to the humble relationship humans had with Him in the Garden of Eden.

God loves humility, and He hates pride. Jesus illustrated humility when He walked on this Earth. Is it any surprise humility represents the antithesis of what Satan values? If you want to stand in the way of Satan's work in this world, then, just as Jesus did, obey the Lord God, pursue humility, and encourage others to do the same.

GOD SEEKS OUT THOSE PEOPLE WILLING TO EXCHANGE THEIR PRIDEFUL LIVING TO RETURN TO THE HUMBLE RELATIONSHIP HUMANS HAD WITH HIM IN THE GARDEN OF EDEN.

God knows a humble heart desires to please Him. *Open to confession, a malleable heart bravely steps out of the elephant sin hiding place.*

Moving Away from Distorted Worship

We begin to build our hiding place because our pride refuses to own up to our disobedience. The secret places we create weigh us down, become uncomfortable and painful, and steal any joy we might have. Here's what Tim Chester wrote:

> One of the main ways in which pride wrecks the process of change occurs when we hide our sin from others...We want our good reputation. So we hide, we pretend, we don't seek help...We want to avoid exposure, so we tell ourselves we can manage on our own. But here's what's really happening: We love our reputation more than we hate our sin.[6]

Pride stands as the source of the idols of your life...your distorted value system. Are you thinking you have no idols? Ask the Holy Spirit to reveal them and then look and listen for the answer, which might surprise you. Knowing where your idols live begins the first step out of hiding.

Katherine and I both pursued a distorted worship, but God called us both out of that place. He can do the same thing for you. In love, God wants to lead you away from the idols you worship now, and He wants you to know His love and the refuge He promises.

Freedom and joy wait for you in God's hiding place. If distorted worship drives you into hiding, you need to pursue true worship, focused on God. He desires you to hide in the refuge He offers. *Freedom and joy don't exist inside our secret place...only outside of it.*

Let's head in that direction.

For Discussion

1. Proverbs 8:13 tells us that God hates pride, arrogance, and evil, and that we should do the same. Why do you think it is difficult to share God's hatred of these three things?

_____

_____

_____

_____

_____

_____

2. We know from 1 Peter 5:5 that God "opposes the proud, but gives grace to the humble." Have you ever felt as if God either opposed you because of your pride, or gave you grace because of humility?

_____

_____

_____

_____

_____

_____

3. In what way does your pride cause you to compare your life to others? Reflect on comparing yourself to others and God's provision for your life. (Check out Hebrews 13:5.)

_____

_____

_____

_____

_____

_____

4. Has it ever occurred to you that you worshipped an idol of some sort? (See Isaiah 37:18-19.) Share some of those thoughts.

_____

_____

_____

_____

_____

_____

5. After reading about how an elephant sin develops in a person's life, share about a small sin that has grown much larger in your life than you ever expected it would. (See Ephesians 5:15-16.)

_____

_____

_____

_____

_____

_____

CHAPTER 3

TRUE WORSHIP

And how will anyone go and tell them without being sent? That is why the Scriptures say, "How beautiful are the feet of messengers who bring good news!"

Romans 10:15 NLT

"**H**EY, MARK, HOW are you feeling today? I imagine you're pretty sore, right?"

"Sore, why would I be sore?"

"Dude, you don't remember? Last night at your house party, you slid down the staircase bannister and landed on your butt like a ton of bricks!

"Wow, I've got no recollection of that! Did I take anyone down with me??"

Yup...one Sunday morning in the 1970s I had this conversation with a college buddy. In my hedonistic college days, I lived in the "Calle Fresno House," known to be Party Central after most home football games (and any other excuse). Back then, I worshipped myself and my desires. Yes, I often went to church on Sunday, but if you saw video clips from my exploits on Saturday night, you would see how much I loved "the world"...*my world*. I lived a life embedded in an I Worship Me paradigm.

I worshipped other gods on Saturday night. I wouldn't have thought of myself as an enemy of God, but according to James 4:4, I lived as one: "So, you are not loyal to God! You should know that loving the world is the same as hating God. Anyone who wants to be a friend of the world becomes God's enemy" (James 4:4 NCV).

My rebellion caused a separation from God: "It's your sins that have cut you off from God. Because of your sins, He has turned away and will not listen anymore" (Isaiah 59:2 NLT). I acted just the same as Adam and Eve did when they made the self-determined decision to pursue what they wanted for themselves. Their disobedience caused an immediate separation from God, and since that time, we have proven the truth, we sin every day: "For all have sinned and fall short of the glory of God" (Romans 3:23).

IF YOU AREN'T MOVING TOWARD GOD, THEN YOU'RE MOVING AWAY FROM HIM.

How does a nice Lutheran boy *unwittingly* become an enemy of God? I'm being gracious by using the term "unwittingly." I didn't start out *desiring* to be an enemy of God, but I knew better than to pursue my life choices. I knew God hated my lifestyle, but I didn't care enough to change. I pursued self-gratification as an idol, and I turned my back on pursuing God. Axiom of life: If you aren't moving toward God, then you're moving away from Him. There's no standing still when it comes to God.

We live as broken, self-centered people, and we refuse to seek God on our own: "The LORD looks down from heaven on the children of man, to see if there are any who understand, who seek after God.

They have all turned aside; together they have become corrupt; there is none who does good, not even one" (Psalm 14:2-3).

Sounds pretty hopeless, right? But God provided a way back to Him. Here's what Jesus said: "The Father sent Me. No man can come to Me unless the Father gives him the desire to come to Me. Then I will raise him to life on the last day" (John 6:44 NLV). So on our own, we won't seek out God unless God causes us to have that desire in our hearts. Considering where my life has been, I am so grateful God sought me out and drew me to Him.

SELF-CENTERED

In the entire universe, God is the most self-centered being of all. Is this a most outrageous statement? Maybe it sounds better this way: In the entire universe, God is the most God-centered. Sounds better, right? Why would it be good for Him to be so focused on Himself? He is the pinnacle of wisdom, love, and moral good. Nothing in the universe compares to Him. For  God to give anything or anyone else more honor than Himself would be evil. God's not capable of sinning.

This causes God to be a jealous god: *"I will rescue you for my sake -yes, for my own sake! I will not let my reputation be tarnished, and I will not share my glory with idols!"* (Isaiah 48:11 NLT). God understands He is the only being who should be honored or worshipped, and so He makes it clear that *all the glory for everything belongs to Him.*

God expects us to understand His worthiness, and He has made this clear in the first two commands of His Ten Commandments:

I am Jehovah your God who liberated you from your slavery in Egypt. "You may worship no other god than me. "You shall not make yourselves any idols: no images of animals, birds, or fish. You must never bow or worship it in any way; for I, the LORD your God, am very possessive. I will not share your affection with any other god! "And when I punish people for their sins, the punishment continues upon the children, grandchildren, and great-grandchildren of those who hate me; but I lavish my love upon thousands of those who love me and obey my commandments (Exodus 20:2-6 TLB).

So God honors Himself, and He commands us to honor Him with our lives as well. Our rebellious side might ask: "Who is God to make demands like this?" Well, here's the answer: He's God, we aren't, He created us, we didn't, He knows what's best for us, and we don't. Isn't that enough?

You might have heard this before: *God's heart is for our good, and for His glory.* He wants nothing but the best for us, and He is the best. He deserves to get all of our glory.

THE GIFT

So God is a jealous God who hates sin, and we're all broken. On the surface, this doesn't put us in a great place with God. But from the beginning, God had a plan to redeem us from our desperate situation. Like Adam and Eve, we can thank God for His mercy (mercy = not giving us what we deserve): "For the wages of sin is death, but the free gift of God is eternal life in Christ Jesus our Lord" (Romans 6:23). Note how the inspired Apostle Paul wrote that line...wages are something *earned*, and we did nothing to earn the gift of salvation.

God gives this free gift to anyone who seeks to receive it. *No one can earn it.*

God offers the gift while we *actively live as God-haters,* or at least we hate being obedient to Him: "But God showed His great love for us by sending Christ to die for us while we were still sinners" (Romans 5:8 NLT). Accepting the gift changes everything in our relationship with God. We go from being an enemy of God, to becoming a child of God: "While we were God's enemies, He made us His friends through the death of His Son. Surely, now that we are His friends, He will save us through His Son's life" (Romans 5:10 NCV).

GOD THE SEEKER

God's heart for His lost children is shown in Ezekiel: *"For thus says the Lord GOD: Behold, I, I myself will search for my sheep and will seek them out"* (Ezekiel 34:11). God seeks out those who will follow Him, giving Him the glory He deserves. He wants to embrace His kids who willingly worship Him. When Adam and Eve hid in shame, the God of the

GOD SEEKS OUT THOSE WHO WILL FOLLOW HIM, GIVING HIM THE GLORY HE DESERVES.

Universe came looking for them, and He came in love. God didn't shame them, but consequences follow disobedience.

In chapter six, we will look at the story of the Prodigal Son. In this parable, Jesus revealed the heart of God as a father who looks for the return of a wayward child. We must make the turn toward God, and when we do, He eagerly brings us to a place of redemption: "Come close to God and He will come close to you. Wash your hands, you sinners. Clean up your hearts, you who want to follow the sinful ways of the world and God at the same time" (James 4:8 NLV).

F.Y.I., don't let this verse lead you to believe you have to have *your whole life* cleaned up before God will accept you. God seeks and saves people who pursue paths leading away from Him, and He will do this at any point in a wayward person's life.

How Did God Redeem Us?

Romans 3:24 says Christ's death for our evil ways allowed us to be "justified" with God. Another way to think of the word *justified* would be, "just as if we had not sinned." Those who accept the free gift of Jesus's death for the forgiveness of their wrongdoing move from death to life because Jesus's sacrifice of Himself causes us to be reconciled to God. We go from being dead in our sins to being alive in Christ.

Followers of Christ have been redeemed by His death. The definition of *redeem* is "to gain or regain possession of something in exchange for payment." God required Jesus's death on the cross as the payment for all of my wrongs and for yours as well. The payment for our brokenness cost Jesus His life, but we are offered the benefit of His death for free. It's a gift freely offered, but if you accept the gift, you will pay with your life. *You will be trading a temporal life focused on you for an eternal life focused on Christ.*

Eden and Heaven Mirrored

Heaven is a perfect place, just like the Garden of Eden God created for Adam and Eve. When God's first children rebelled, He had to remove them from that place, because He couldn't tolerate imperfection there.

Heaven is the same. You aren't welcome in heaven if you are 99.99999999% good. God has every right to demand perfection in His heaven, since He created it all. Only if you accept the free gift of Jesus Christ's death for your sinful pursuits will God welcome you into an eternity with Him. When you accept Jesus's sacrificial blood as the covering for your errors, you are then seen by God as 100% pure because Jesus is the only perfect sacrifice that would satisfy God.

YOU HAVE A CHOICE

If you haven't yet accepted Christ as your Savior and made Him the Lord of your life, then right now, you might not know it, but you live as an enemy of God, and you face a life and death choice. One choice will lead you to freedom and eternal life because you accept Jesus has paid for your wrongs, and you have decided to receive the free gift. If you reject the gift, then you will be choosing to pay the price by yourself for all of your misdeeds.

ONLY IF YOU ACCEPT THE FREE GIFT OF JESUS CHRIST'S DEATH FOR YOUR SINFUL PURSUITS WILL GOD WELCOME YOU INTO AN ETERNITY WITH HIM.

Don't underestimate the weight of the last sentence. Don't read anything else until you grasp everything it means.

God judges all sin, and He punishes all sin. Deciding you have no need for Jesus as your Savior means when you die, you will stand before God, and no one will be in your corner defending you against the wrath of God. You will have decided you can defend yourself.

Most often, people have a mistaken understanding about how God judges our faults. For some reason, they think God has some kind of giant scale to weigh the good and bad deeds a person has done. They assume if the scale tips anywhere close to the good side, then God will let them into His heaven.

Not so much.

Years ago, I went to Russia on a number of church planting mission trips, and we went door-to-door to share the good news of Jesus. We had an interpreter with us who translated our English into

Russian. When sharing with Russian people, I would often say, "Across the world, many people think God weighs our good and bad deeds." Then I would make hand motions  as if weighing something on a balance scale, and I could see people's eyes light up in understanding and agreement there was truth to that concept.

Sorry, it's just not true...not for Americans, Russians, or anyone else in the world. God has no balance scale, and if He did, our wrongs would far outweigh any good we might have done.

MAKING THE RIGHT CHOICE

You might be asking: *"How do I make this choice? How can I accept the gift Jesus offers?"* It's simple: Believe, confess, and obey.

"For God so loved the world, that He gave His only Son, that whoever believes in Him should not perish but have eternal life" (John 3:16). The first step is to believe. But, you might ask, what am I supposed to believe?

The Apostle Paul wrote the most clear statement for us in Romans: "If you say with your mouth that Jesus is Lord, and believe in your heart that God raised Him from the dead, you will be saved from the punishment of sin. When we believe in our hearts, we are made right with God. We tell with our mouth how we were saved from the punishment of sin" (Romans 10:9-10 NLV). Paul encourages you to change your heart's attitude about Jesus, accept His gift, and confess your faith in what Jesus did on the cross for your disobedience.

Your belief in Jesus as Savior makes you "right with God." You have been justified...as if you had not sinned. I know this sounds unbelievable, but God forgives *all the wrongs you have committed or will commit.* Your confession of your faith in Christ testifies of your salvation. But it doesn't end there. If you have accepted Jesus as your

Savior, the Holy Spirit comes to dwell in your heart. He will encourage you to live like Jesus, and He will enable you to change from the inside out.

DECISION TIME

You have a decision to make. You have heard the good news of Jesus Christ, and the redemption He offers through His death. Will you respond and accept His offer, or will you walk away and leave His offer on the table?

WILL YOU RESPOND AND ACCEPT HIS OFFER, OR WILL YOU WALK AWAY AND LEAVE HIS OFFER ON THE TABLE?

If you have made a decision to follow Christ, please tell a trusted friend you've decided to dedicate your life to Jesus. Accountability is powerful.

THINGS GOTTA CHANGE

We saw a whole lot of people in Russia who prayed to receive Jesus as their Savior, but year after year, only small changes occurred in the local Russian church. Few people changed the way they lived. They didn't obey. Their lives did not conform to God's Word. Don't think this is only true of Russia. This is true in America and across the world. Pride stands in the way of change.

A changed life reveals the Holy Spirit at work. When the Holy Spirit "convicts" or "convinces" a person about sinful ways, the evidence must be a changed life: "But the fruit of the Spirit is love, joy, peace, patience, kindness, goodness, faithfulness, gentleness, self-control" (Galatians 5:22-23a). Those traits show evidence of a redeemed life and a renewed mind, focused on transformation and living for God.

A New Creation with an Old Shadow

As followers of Christ, we live as a *new creation*. Do we constantly feel like a new creation? No, but we can be assured we are. The Apostle Paul tells us in 2 Corinthians 5:17: "Therefore, if anyone is in Christ, he is a new creation. The old has passed away; behold, the new has come."

The *old self* we were before we followed Jesus no longer exists. That old self is who we were when we lived as an enemy of God. Though we live as a new creation, God allowed a reminder to exist of who we were in the past. The Bible calls that our "flesh." Today, our flesh exists in constant conflict with our new redeemed self.

The writer of the book of Hebrews talks about the struggle we have with our flesh and our habitual disobedience:

> Since we have such a huge crowd of men of faith watching us from the grandstands, let us strip off anything that slows us down or holds us back, and especially those sins that wrap themselves so tightly around our feet and trip us up; and let us run with patience the particular race that God has set before us (Hebrews 12:1 TLB).

Sins that "wrap themselves so tightly around our feet and trip us up" sound like a shadow hanging around our feet. Let's think of that shadow as our flesh. We can't get away from our shadow while walking outside on a sunny day, and in this life, we can't get rid of our flesh that leads us into rebellion.

When Paul wrote the book of Romans, he shared his struggle: "For I do not do the good I want, but the evil I do not want is what I keep on doing" (Romans 7:19). Now if the man who wrote almost half of the books of the New Testament complains that he doesn't get it right, then you're definitely not alone.

Followers of Christ who live out their faith in obedience to God's Word will not be free of this conflict, but hope exists to battle it.

> Now the works of the flesh are evident: sexual immorality, impurity, sensuality, idolatry, sorcery, enmity, strife, jealousy, fits of anger, rivalries, dissensions, divisions, envy, drunkenness, orgies, and things like these. I warn you, as I warned you before, that those who do such things will not inherit the kingdom of God (Galatians 5:19-21).

Somewhere in that list I'm sure you can find some of your personal "fleshly shadow." Those sins clinging to you show the bits of darkness that still hang around after the lights of Christ's redemption came on.

CO-OPERATION

When I learned to drive, our high school had a car designed for Driver's Ed. The car was a typical 4-door sedan, except it had another brake pedal for the instructor. That pedal could be used if the instructor needed to make an emergency stop. Although I've only seen  pictures, some driver's education cars have a second steering wheel, so the instructor can take control of the entire vehicle.

Let's use that kind of vehicle as an illustration of the conflict between our flesh and the Holy Spirit. When we become followers of Christ, the Holy Spirit climbs into the "driver's seat of our lives," and we slide over into the passenger seat. We will "co-operate" our lives with the Holy Spirit.

What does that look like on a daily basis? The Holy Spirit encourages and convicts us in making godly decisions about the direction we should be going. As we become accustomed to cooperating with the Holy Spirit, we will understand more about godly thinking, and how we need to change our words and actions to mirror our godly thoughts.

Our flesh likes to yank the steering wheel away and take us in an ungodly direction, but our redeemed self doesn't want to go that way anymore. In his book *The Enemy Within*, Kris Lundgaard writes: "Since the believer is born of the sin-hating Spirit, he can never give himself to sin fully, absolutely, the way an unbeliever can... Just as the flesh resists every spiritual act, the Spirit resists every sin."[7]

OUR FLESH LIKES TO YANK THE STEERING WHEEL AWAY AND TAKE US IN AN UNGODLY DIRECTION, BUT OUR REDEEMED SELF DOESN'T WANT TO GO THAT WAY ANYMORE.

Our redeemed self wants to live a life that shows I Worship God. We need to be intentional about gripping our steering wheel of life to pull in the direction the Holy Spirit leads. How do we do that? We need to renew our minds so we hear His directions better.

When we cooperate with the Holy Spirit, we will be doing what Paul encourages in Galatians: "But I say, walk by the Spirit, and you will not gratify the desires of the flesh. For the desires of the flesh are against the Spirit, and the desires of the Spirit are against the flesh, for these are opposed to each other, to keep you from doing the things you want to do" (Galatians 5:16-17).

REDEMPTION IN A NUTSHELL

The Bible often talks about Jesus as being a Redeemer, because He came to Earth to redeem humans from the penalty we owe for our disobedience. Jesus's sacrifice of Himself on the cross satisfied God's punishment for our wrongs. If it's unclear how you can accept Jesus as your Savior (or Redeemer) and Lord, it's not hard. There are three changes you have to make.

1. Change your heart

2. Change your mind

3. Change your actions

The first step is to agree you live a broken life…every day you pursue sinful things, both big and small. *Your heart needs to grieve over your rebellion against God.* This kind of rebellion makes you His enemy.

The second step is to change your mind about who will be the lord of your life. To be redeemed, you must decide to make Jesus your Lord. This second step hits your pride hard, because it means *you have to sacrifice your agenda for God's agenda.*

The final step is to move away from the disobedient actions which separate you from God. *You need to put off your actions that offend God, and you need to put on righteous actions.* The road gets rougher here because the first two steps only require you to think differently. Step three is difficult because you have to act differently. You have to make different choices in your actions, and then continue living those choices out.

These changes can only occur because your mind is being renewed every day. You have to begin to think and act differently than you've thought or acted before. The good news is you now have a

Helper. If you turn your life over to Jesus, He promises to send His Holy Spirit to live in you, and to cause change from the inside out.

God-Centered

People who follow Jesus still mess up in many of the same ways they did before making Christ their Lord, but daily they work alongside the Holy Spirit to change to be more God-centered people. Turning from distorted worship toward true worship of God causes the transformation into I Worship God people.

God is God-centered, and we want to be the same. Christ's loving sacrifice of Himself on the cross took us out of the darkness as an enemy of God and made us children of God. "He has delivered us from the domain of darkness and transferred us to the kingdom of his beloved Son, in whom we have redemption, the forgiveness of sins" (Col. 1:13-14).

God deserves the daily sacrifice of our self-focus because through His Son, He provided a way to find peace with Him. When we know peace in the community of faith in Christ, everything changes. We find out we aren't alone. We realize everyone has been hiding something, and we have great hope of freedom knowing we have let God's Light into our dark places.

You're not alone.
Everyone has a hiding place.
Hope is in letting God's Light in.

For Discussion

1. In James 4:4 we read a "friend of the world" can become an enemy of God. Share about a time in your life when you lived as a friend of the world. Was it fun for a time? Do you have regrets?

_____

_____

_____

_____

_____

_____

2. God says He will search for His sheep in Ezekial 34:11. If you are a follower of Christ, share about how God sought you out.

_____

_____

_____

_____

_____

_____

3. Romans 6:23 teaches that God offers a free gift of salvation. Share why you believe people have a difficult time accepting that free gift.

_____

_____

_____

_____

_____

_____

4. In Romans 10:9-10 it seems as if salvation is quite simple: *believe, confess, and obey.* If you have not yet accepted Jesus as your Savior, what do you think is holding you back?

_____

_____

_____

_____

_____

_____

5. We know from Galatians 5:16-17 people who receive Christ as their Savior will exhibit fruits of the Spirit. If you are a follower of Christ, share how you see that fruit in your life.

_____

_____

_____

_____

_____

_____

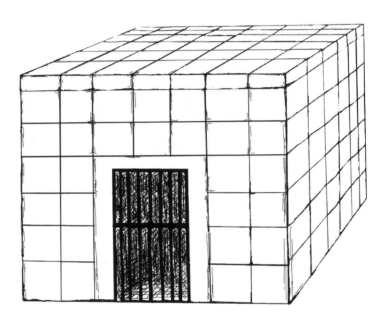

CHAPTER 4

HIDING

All who do evil hate the light and will not come to the light, because it will show all the evil things they do.

John 3:20 NCV

"**S**TOP IT! THAT is so vulgar!" my mom yelled.

At 6 years old, "vulgar" was a new word for me. I didn't know just what it meant, but based on my mom's angry tone, I didn't want to hear it again. In a moment, I figured out "vulgar" wasn't a good thing.

I had just been caught "playing doctor" with the girl next door!

Mom's anger filled the laundry room where she found us. Though I'm vague on the details about the girl or what we were doing, the words, "That is so vulgar" were etched in my memory.

The lady in the doorway wearing a scowl on a bright red face, followed up with, "You should be ashamed!" My own red face revealed my shame and embarrassment, and I wanted to sink through the floor and disappear.

As soon as Mom busted up our laundry room exploits, I felt a deep sense of guilt and shame. Five minutes before, I didn't realize our behavior was that wrong, but my mom's tone of voice, and the new word I just learned, told me we were doing something which shouldn't be done at all.

KNOWING RIGHT FROM WRONG

Even at 6, I made a morally wrong decision, and my mom had every right to call me out. I needed guidance, and I needed discipleship in my decisions and actions. My youth and inexperience shouldn't have gotten me off the hook for my responsibility to make right choices. I needed to know how to live an I Worship God life.

But how do we know what's right and wrong? I imagine the girl from next door and I knew something about right from wrong, or why would we have hidden away in the laundry room? From birth, all of us have been given the blessing of a conscience. Our conscience shows we have an internal knowledge why some choices are right, and others are wrong. One analogy for the conscience could be a traffic signal which indicates "Go," "Stop," or "Caution." We have a conscience because God created us in His image. God's righteous fingerprint on our lives is revealed in our conscience.

WHEN WE FACE TEMPTATION TO DO WRONG, OUR CONSCIENCE SHOULD LIGHT UP A "CAUTION" OR "STOP" LIGHT TO POINT US IN A DIFFERENT DIRECTION.

When we face temptation to do wrong, our conscience should light up a "Caution" or "Stop" light to point us in a different direction. If our conscience has not matured, it's in need of training. When my mom stopped me from playing doctor, she informed my conscience of my wrongdoing. This new information helped to strengthen my conscience toward godly behavior. Young, immature consciences grow in a manner similar to how bodybuilders rely on protein and exercise to build muscle. Like protein for our consciences, the moral influence of God's Word, and positive, intentional parenting (discipling) form the primary building blocks of a strong, clear conscience. As we learn more of the truth of God's Word (protein), and we put this truth into practice (exercise), our consciences grow stronger.

If growing godly character is our goal, a strong conscience is foundational. A strong conscience helps us become more discerning in our decision-making and will keep us at a distance from doing wrong. But when we secretly coddle a sin and cover it up, we create a stronghold, which I did in my pattern of weak self-control. Like concrete, these patterns harden into a hiding place.

How We Build Our Hiding Place

From early in our lives we exhibit a desire to serve ourselves more than serving God or the needs of others. Our pride-driven nature wants to fulfill its desires, and it takes some schooling to become aware of how to humbly serve.

In chapter 2, we learned we conceal our ugly stuff because of pride. You will notice my illustration includes a throne on top of a prideful foundation. The throne represents the worship we give to our desires. This distorted worship of ourselves and our passions draws us away from worshipping God.

GUILT

When we disobey God, we feel guilty because *we are guilty*. Guilt shapes us in spiritually healthy ways, because it's a clue we have strayed off God's path. The question becomes, what do we do with our guilt? Guilt signals a fork in the road. We have a choice to make of either moving toward God through confession, or away from God into fear and hiding. If we choose fear and hiding, just like Adam and Eve, we have succumbed to Satan's lies about an angry, unloving, and untrustworthy God.

Taking responsibility for our wrongs through confession plays an essential role in our transformation. God promises to forgive our offenses, but we have to confess them to Him. If you aren't familiar with the practice of confession, then here's a simple definition: *you agree with God about your sin.* You acknowledge you disobeyed God's laws or commandments. *Confession of our wrongdoing requires talking about it, both to God and others.*

Rick Warren writes in *The Purpose Driven Life*: "The truth is, whatever you can't talk about is already out of control in your life; problems with your finances, marriage, kids, thoughts, sexuality, secret habits, or anything else. If you could handle it on your own, you would have already done so. But you can't. Will power and personal resolutions aren't enough."[8]

Our pride fights against confession because agreeing with God about our brokenness requires humility. We feel guilty when our thoughts or our actions come into conflict with righteous internal values. For believers, those internal values help us to understand what God expects of us, and what we expect of ourselves.

If we allow it, feeling guilt before God has the ability to lead us to *godly sorrow* (sorrow before God because of sin). Many times, though, we just feel bad we hurt someone else, and we don't want to feel the consequences of wrongdoing in our relationships. We may feel guilty before others and judged by them. We call this reaction *worldly sorrow* (sorrow before other humans because we sinned against them).

When we don't confess to God, we put up the first wall of our hiding place. We start to construct the place where we begin to accumulate our unconfessed sin, and we start construction of the *wall of guilt*.

CONVICTION VS. CONDEMNATION

Before Christ died, He promised He would send us a Helper, His Holy Spirit, to live in us. Here's what Jesus said about the work of the Holy Spirit: "And when He comes, He (the Holy Spirit) will convict the world concerning sin and righteousness and judgment: concerning sin, because they do not believe in me" (John 16:8-9). Conviction is one of the jobs of the Holy Spirit. Through conviction, we become "convinced" of our guilt. We agree with God our actions or our thoughts were bad; they were wrong.

Author Edward T. Welch writes: "One way that God loves his people is by sending his Spirit to convict the world of guilt in regard to sin (John 16:8-11). This is not condemnation; it is God's way of rescuing us. Sin is a path that leads to tragedy and despair. If someone saw you on that path and did nothing, *that* would be unloving. But the Spirit of God awakens our hearts to the presence of sin in our lives, and then convinces us that He forgives sins because of Jesus Christ and gives us peace. It is when we experience *no* conviction of sin that we should be most alarmed."[9]

SATAN DOESN'T LIKE YOU TO BE *CONVICTED* OF YOUR WRONGS, BECAUSE HE KNOWS THAT WILL HEAD YOU BACK *TOWARD GOD*.

Satan doesn't like you to be *convicted of* your wrongs, because he knows that will head you back *toward God*. He wants you to feel *condemnation*, which he knows will cause you to distance yourself from God. Don't let Satan get away with this. You've got to call him out as a liar.

The God who came searching for Adam and Eve promises if you confess, you will not be condemned: "There is therefore now no condemnation for those who are in Christ Jesus. For the law of the Spirit of life has set you free in Christ Jesus from the law of sin and death" (Romans 8:1-2).

WITHOUT TRUST, FEAR MAKES US HIDE MORE

Fear caused Adam and Eve to want to conceal themselves from God. In their defense, we need to remember they had no idea what God would do once they sinned. God said they would die, but did He mean right away? Without previous experience, Adam and Eve didn't know God's nature extends grace, mercy, and forgiveness. *Fortunately, we are blessed to know that God.*

Let's consider what frightens us most, because this is a huge reason behind the covering up of our secrets. When it comes to our relationship with God, we often don't trust God's love, and we fear He will punish or condemn us. This comes from listening to Satan's lying whispers about God's love and trustworthiness.

We feel added anxiety in our relationships with other people because we fear the revelation of our brokenness will change how they relate to us.

Pride-driven fear tries to protect us emotionally from more guilt, and from the shame coming around the corner. Without confession comes greater pain, and then we begin building the next wall of our hiding place, the *wall of fear*.

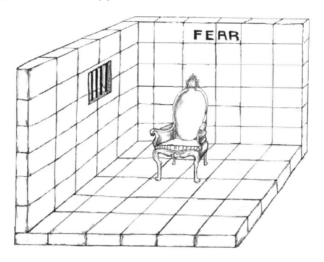

THE MAGIC THIEF

At the age of 8, I loved magic so intensely I stole money from my father's "change box" to buy more tricks. One day, my mom took me to a novelty store, and I bought a new trick with my ill-gotten change. I think the cost of the trick I bought raised some flags with my mom. When we got home, she questioned me about how I could afford the trick and I buckled. The truth came out.

"I took the money from Dad's change box to buy it," I confessed.

The words barely left my mouth, and my mom had her car keys in her hand. She dragged me out of the house and pushed me toward the car.

"We're going back to the store, and YOU will have some explaining to do to the store manager," she said.

She might as well have been driving me to the police station to have me booked for armed robbery. I started crying and pleading with her.

I couldn't reason with her. When we got back to the store, I tried to make myself disappear, but when I opened my eyes, I still stood in the same spot my mom had planted me.

As the manager approached, I couldn't bear to look at him. Tears welled up in my eyes, because of my shame and embarrassment in being hauled into such a public place to give my confession.

"I stole money from my dad to pay for this trick," I blurted out, as I held up the stolen goods. That incident embedded itself into my memory. Just like being caught playing doctor, my guilt, shame, and embarrassment intensified the moment, and engraved it into my brain.

SHAME...A CANCEROUS EMOTION

If we refuse to take responsibility for our wrongdoing, we can internalize all that ever-growing guilt and begin to feel a sense of personal unworthiness. Deep down, we feel badly about ourselves internally. Those intense feelings create the essence of shame.

Stephen Pattison writes this about the difference between guilt and shame: "Guilty people feel that they have done *some specific thing*

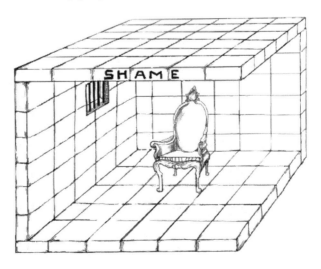

that is wrong or bad; their shamed counterparts have to face an unbearable sense that *their whole self is bad.*"[10]

We can feel shame for a lot of reasons. Some of the issues causing deeper feelings of shame for Christ followers can be abortion, adultery, pornography, same sex attraction, and pre-marital sex. When we have done things that reveal we don't match up to who we think we are or how we want to be perceived by others, we can be left feeling awful.

The shame covers the place where we hide. Covering our wrongs seems important to us so no one else can see them (including God, we foolishly think). But God has great patience, grace, love, and mercy.

He wants us to turn away from building our hiding place and seek His forgiveness. We need His grace and mercy to cover our unrighteousness and our shame. If we accept God's grace, and trust in His mercy, we won't feel the need to cover up.

EMBARRASSMENT

Embarrassment over wrongdoing makes us want to run away from other people, and it happens when our bad stuff goes public. We feel all eyes focused on us, everyone knows we screwed up, and the *wall of embarrassment* forms. Embarrassment should be a normal reaction to our wrongdoing, and yet, today we see signs of hearts hardened

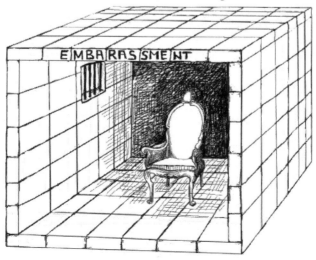

to shame. A lack of embarrassment reveals hearts that agree with Satan…sin is not a big deal.

Edward Welch is one of my favorite contemporary Christian writers. From his book *Shame Interrupted* he writes, "If you are still stuck, check for hidden sins or sins you have confessed but are *already planning to commit again.* With hidden sins, track down a wise person and bring that sin into the light. That will at least get you moving in the right direction. With confessed but cherished sins you plan to repeat, the issue is not shame before God but its opposite: shamelessness."[11]

If you look at social media today, many in our society have become less ashamed and less embarrassed by how they live out their lives. As Jeremiah wrote, "they don't even know how to blush" (Jeremiah 6:15).

LOVE OF DARKNESS

Scripture often contrasts the Light of God with darkness, and it tells us we have a tendency to prefer darkness to cover our evil ways.

> And the judgment is based on this fact: God's light came into the world, but people loved the darkness more than the light, for their actions were evil. All who do evil hate the light and refuse to go near it for fear their sins will be exposed (John 3:19-20 NLT).

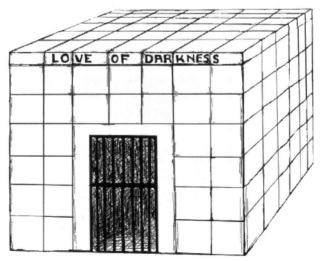

We like the darkness because it feels safe from the spotlight on our wrongdoing. Let's face it. Sin can feel good...for a moment. Fallen people like you and me can experience temporary pleasure in disobeying God, and we can develop a rebellious lifestyle. Why is that?

Galatians 5 says those desires of our flesh are set against the Spirit of God, and the desires include sexual immorality, impurity, sensuality, idolatry, sorcery, enmity, strife, jealousy, fits of anger, rivalries, dissensions, divisions, envy, drunkenness, orgies, and things like these.

Now I haven't participated in an orgy, or in sorcery, but my flesh has felt the guilt of all the rest of this sad list. If you're honest about your life, and your willingness to follow your fleshly pursuits, these desires might ring a bell for you, too.

When we add the *wall of darkness*, we complete our hiding place, and we remove ourselves from God and others. For so many reasons, this seclusion takes a toll on our lives, and we feel lonely. We "hole up" as captives in a place of our making, and our usefulness in fulfilling God's great plans for our lives diminishes.

Dietrich Bonhoeffer was a pastor, theologian, and writer in the early 20th century. He was executed at the young age of 39 in a Nazi concentration camp. Bonhoeffer's writings are rich with encouragement for the Christian community of faith, and he often wrote about the loneliness of a secret life: "The more lonely people become, the more destructive the power of sin over them...Sin wants to remain unknown. It shuns the light. In the darkness of what is left unsaid, sin poisons the whole being of a person."[12]

THE ILLUSION OF SAFETY

When we complete our hiding place, we live under the illusion that no one, including God, can see us there. We fool ourselves into believing we are safe; however, we are anything but that.

I don't think any of us start out with the intention of building a place such as this, but like raising an elephant inside our home, we just slide into a bigger problem. We start by covering up something small, which turns into a huge issue in our life.

What begins as a simple temptation turns into something like a temple. It's where we worship things other than God. We serve the lusts of our flesh there instead of the God whom we should be serving.

With the help of the Holy Spirit, let's work on tearing apart these hiding places. Letting the Spirit illuminate our dark place is the only way to overcome our fear, live in freedom, and find our true Kingdom purpose.

God can heal us from all forms of sin and shame. He wants us to feel His forgiveness, but that only happens when we no longer hide. *The destruction of our hiding place, with its shame, guilt, and fear, happens when we take responsibility for our habitual wrongdoing. Once we have shouldered responsibility, we can lay it before God in confession, and we can lay it before friends who we count on to hold us accountable.*

You Can't Hide in Two Places at Once

Our broken ways that we cover up stand in the way of living in the secure and strong refuge God provides. We can't have it both ways. We can't worship our idols and worship God. We can't be hiding in the shelter of God's sacred tent and cowering in the hiding place we create at the same time.

OFTEN, WE DON'T TRUST GOD BECAUSE WE CAN'T UNDERSTAND HOW HE COULD LOVE PEOPLE LIKE US.

The only safe place lies in the protection, sanctuary, and refuge of God, but we often turn our backs on this protection for one or more reasons:

- *We are afraid of God*
- *We don't trust God*
- *We don't think we need God*

Let's look closer at this faulty thinking:

We have a fear of God because we assume He will reject us. Our guilt and shame (along with Satan's whispers) drive us to this place. But the truths revealed in Scripture don't support this perspective.

Often, we don't trust God because we can't understand how He could love people like us. God has a great plan for our lives, but to pursue His plan, we need to trust Him more than we trust ourselves. We need to trust His grace, mercy, and forgiveness.

Pridefully, many of us think we can find our way apart from God. How deluded we are. God has unlimited wisdom, and He wants to share with us His best path for us to follow. We fool ourselves by thinking we could craft a better plan than God's.

We can't build a safe refuge for ourselves. If we want freedom from guilt and shame, we must seek out the refuge of God.

> One thing I ask from the LORD, this only do I seek: that I may dwell in the house of the LORD all the days of my life, to gaze on the beauty of the LORD and to seek Him in His temple. For in the day of trouble He will keep me safe in His dwelling; He will hide me in the shelter of His sacred tent and set me high upon a rock (Psalm 27:4-5 NIV).

God proclaims how He delivers us from our troubles.

> How great is the goodness you have stored up for those who fear you. You lavish it on those who come to you for

protection, blessing them before the watching world. You hide them in the shelter of your presence, safe from those who conspire against them. You shelter them in your presence, far from accusing tongues (Psalm 31:19-20 NLT).

SHOUTS OF DELIVERANCE

Since the Fall and the entrance of evil into His Creation, God desires we would see Him as our refuge. Just listen as King David writes with reverence of our God as a place of peace and safety: "You are a hiding place for me; you preserve me from trouble you surround me with shouts of deliverance" (Psalm 32:7).

Can you imagine a God who surrounds you with *shouts of deliverance*? He often surrounds us by the voices of His other followers, others in the church. John Bevere writes in his book *The Bait of Satan*: "God never created us to live separately and independently

CAN YOU IMAGINE A GOD WHO SURROUNDS YOU WITH *SHOUTS OF DELIVERANCE*?

of each other. He likes it when His children care for and nurture each other...He wants us to be active members of the family."[13]

THERE'S GOOD NEWS AHEAD

There's good news for everyone: You don't need to cover up your wrongs. But here's your greatest challenge: stuffing your pride and humbly accepting the fact you need to 1) fear an awesome, loving God, 2) trust Him with all of your wrongs, and 3) realize you need God as your Savior and your Lord. God loves you though you have hidden stuff. I know you may not feel this way, but it's the truth. If you have been led to believe otherwise, then I need to call that out as a lie. It's a lie from the enemy of your soul. It's not from God.

To combat the lies of Satan, you don't need to look any further than the Scriptures. *God put everything you need to know in writing for a purpose: to reveal His truths.* The Bible stands as the truth of God's refuge...consider it an invitation to safety and freedom.

We have to trust a loving God who knows who and what we are and loves us anyway. Remember: "He knows how we were made; He remembers that we are dust" (Psalm 103:14 NCV). Also, we need to surround ourselves with other people who own up to their faults, live transparently in confession, and encourage us to do the same.

THE LIGHT BEARER

God, the Creator of the Universe, wants to draw you out of the darkness. He wants this both for your freedom, and for His Glory. When you put off all the ugly stuff you've been hiding you can become all He intends for you to be in His Kingdom. Light dispels darkness. Living in the darkness of our sin creates a form of bondage, and we need to understand we choose this bondage. God's light brings freedom, but we have to partner with Him in seeking that freedom.

Freedom won't happen without you allowing His light to flood into your dark spaces. We tend to think it's not safe to let God into those spaces, but God's plan for our redemption was fulfilled in Jesus Christ, the God-Man who said this: "And whoever sees Me sees Him [God] who sent me. I have come into the world as light, so that whoever believes in me may not remain in darkness" (John 12:45-46).

WRECKING BALL

We need to use a spiritual wrecking ball on our hiding place. We need to demolish that place wall by wall until we get down to its prideful foundation, and if a "humility jackhammer" existed, we need to use it on the prideful foundation.

A heart full of pride rarely pursues change. Only when we remove the foundation of pride will we begin moving toward God's refuge.

Freedom and security live in His hiding place, but we won't know that until we humbly begin to break down the walls we hide behind.

God will not push His way into a place where He isn't wanted, but He wants to bring you into the light. You have to trust Him, and you have to invite Him to shine His Light in your darkness. When you allow Him to do that, you will be amazed at how He will transform you.

Hope is in letting God's light in.

For Discussion

1. One of the primary jobs of the Holy Spirit is to convict humans of their sin. (John 16:8-9) Share your feelings about the Holy Spirit's work. Do you welcome His conviction? Or do you push it away?

_____

_____

_____

_____

_____

_____

2. Romans 8:1-2 teaches us that followers of Christ are not condemned by their sin but have been set free. Yet many Christians live as if they are under a sentence of condemnation. Why do you think this is? Do you think Satan has anything to do with it? Why or why not?

_____

_____

_____

_____

_____

_____

3. Paul's writing in 2 Corinthians 7:10 draws a contrast between godly sorrow and worldly sorrow. Why do you think he says that worldly sorrow leads to death? Share about a time you felt worldly sorrow over your sin instead of godly sorrow.

_____

_____

_____

_____

_____

_____

4. John 3:19-20 points out that people love the darkness because it allows them to hide their wrongs. In John 12:45-46, Jesus says that He came to this world as the Light so others would not remain in darkness. If Jesus came to help illuminate people's lives, why do so many avoid Him?

_____

_____

_____

_____

_____

_____

5. Read Psalm 103:12-14. What do you think King David meant when he wrote the Lord "remembers that we are dust"? Does that statement seem comforting or not?

_____

_____

_____

_____

_____

_____

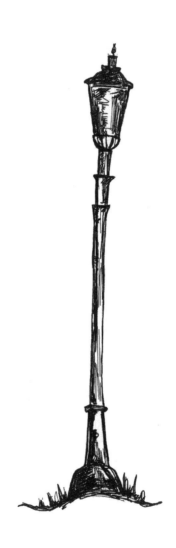

CHAPTER 5

THE PATHWAY

At one time you lived in darkness. Now you are living in
the light that comes from the Lord. Live as children who
have the light of the Lord in them. This light gives us truth.
It makes us right with God and makes us good.

Ephesians 5:8-9 NLV

O N April 26, 2003, Aron Ralston's life changed forever on a hike in Blue John Canyon, Utah. An 800-pound boulder broke loose while Aron worked his way down the slot canyon walls and it fell, pinning Aron's right hand against the rocks.

Aron had been hiking alone and had no way to call anyone for help. No cell phone…nothing. For five days, he attempted to free his arm, but with no success. In desperation, Aron came to realize that, given the limited tools he had, the only way to free himself would be to break both bones in his right forearm, and then cut off his hand.

Can you imagine doing that to yourself…and with no anesthesia? But Aron had to extract himself from his desperate situation or he would die there. Once he twisted his arm sufficiently to break the two bones, it took Aron a full hour to cut off his decaying hand.

When he began the trek out of the canyon eight miles back to his car, he had lost 40 pounds and 25 percent of his blood supply. After amputating his hand, the battle didn't end for Aron. He had to rappel down a 65-foot sheer wall single-handed before he could begin the hike toward his car.

Fortunately for Aron, a family who knew he was missing was hiking in the area and found him stumbling in the desert. One of the family members ran to alert the authorities who were already searching for Aron, and within four hours of cutting off his arm, a helicopter rescue team rushed Aron to a hospital.

Aron Ralston had a difficult choice to make. He could hope he would be rescued before he died of dehydration or he could hope he wouldn't bleed to death after amputating his arm. Radical situations require radical measures.

Radical Heart Surgery

You may need radical surgery, and you may not know it. There's a problem with your heart that has been ignored for years, and it's time to do something. I'm not talking about your physical heart that pumps your blood. I'm referring to your inner being...the core of your thoughts, desires, and motivations. That's where we all have problems. Jay Adams writes:

> There is a belief that man and his actions and his attitudes must be changed at the inner core of his being so that his very set of values and the inner springs of his motivation are affected. The Bible calls this inner power man's heart. It is from the heart that people's problems stem.[14]

We all need surgery on our heart, and the Bible tells us why. Listen to God speaking through the prophet Jeremiah: "The heart is deceitful above all things, and desperately sick; who can understand it?" (Jeremiah 17:9). As we talked about in chapter two, we have a *worship disorder in our heart*. Like Adam and Eve, humans from birth begin with a

WE ALL NEED SURGERY ON OUR HEART, AND THE BIBLE TELLS US WHY

prideful worship of themselves and their desires, and it's like a cancer that has been growing for years.

Let's use a tree with roots as an illustration of a worship disorder in a spiritual heart. Jesus spoke of this analogy in Matthew 7:17-18. If the roots of a fruit tree embed themselves into a deceitful, prideful heart, focused on serving oneself, then the "fruit" (or behavior) the tree produces will be bad because the heart that feeds the tree only concerns itself with fulfilling the lusts of the flesh. The cancer in that heart can metastasize into all areas of thought and action. That cancer needs to be cut out.

But there's hope. I'm sure it won't surprise you to know hope lies in Jesus Christ and the Holy Spirit. If the roots of a tree find their nourishment in a heart that has conformed to the humble model of Christ, then the fruit of that tree will be totally different. The good fruit of that tree will serve God and others.

God desires worship like that. This reveals the humble heart David wrote about in Psalm 51: "The sacrifices of God are a broken spirit; a broken and contrite heart, O God, you will not despise." Broken and contrite hearts begin the transformation God desires.

Jesus and the Holy Spirit- Radical Heart Surgeons

Jesus didn't shy away from using drastic metaphors to teach us how we should deal with our sin. In the book of Matthew, here's what Jesus said about responding to temptation:

> If your right eye causes you to stumble, gouge it out and throw it away. It is better for you to lose one part of your body than for your whole body to be thrown into hell. And if your right hand causes you to stumble, cut it off and throw it away. It is better for you to lose one part of your body than for your whole body to go into hell (Matthew 5:29-30 NIV).

Was Jesus serious about gouging out eyes and cutting off hands? No, but He used this illustration to teach how seriously we need to think about our broken lives. God wants us to take any and all steps to deal with our wrongs. Christ makes the point it's better to live a temporary life deformed, than to live an eternal life apart from Him.

In the book, *Of the Mortification of Sin in Believers,* a seventeenth-century Puritan pastor and author, John Owen, writes about believers "killing" sin. The book digs into just one verse in Romans: "If you do what your sinful old selves want you to do, you will die in sin. But if, through the power of the Holy Spirit, you destroy those actions to which the body can be led, you will have life" (Romans 8:13 NLV).

You hide some things which need to be killed. Remember when we talked about your elephant sin? Those actions need to be destroyed with the help of God's Holy Spirit.

Yes, God's Word calls you to destroy unrighteous habits, but you have help in your struggle. The Holy Spirit of God has been sent to walk with you, and as Dr. John MacArthur writes in his commentary from *The MacArthur Study Bible*: "...the Spirit provides us with the energy and power to continually and gradually be killing our sins, a process never completed in this life. The means the Spirit uses to accomplish this process is our faithful obedience to the simple commands of Scripture."[15]

Killing your elephant sin (the cancer of your heart) requires radical measures, and it begins the process of dealing with our flesh. For many of us, that's a huge challenge. But remember, we have a Helper. Elyse Fitzpatrick writes in her book *Idols of the Heart*: "How do we kill idols?…How can we get rid of what seems to be an intrinsic part of who we are? We can take courage that God's Spirit, who searches hearts, is continually working to enlighten and enable us."[16]

WHERE DO WE BEGIN?

I've been a photographer for over 40 years, and I have an appreciation for controlled lighting. If we want to come out of our secret life and get rid of that shadow of our flesh, we have to focus light on our disobedient flesh and its pursuits. Just like a heart surgeon needs focused light to do his job well, we need to illuminate our hiding place and enlighten ourselves on the pathway out of hiding.

Three lampposts illuminate that path: prayer, meditation on God's Word, and accountability to others. These three lampposts provide the light we need to pursue the pathway out of hiding. Along with light, they act as guardrails, helping to keep us on that path.

LAMPPOST ONE: PRAYER

We need to make prayer a high priority. So often, I am guilty of ignoring opportunities for prayer. But God wants to hear our prayers, especially confessional prayers that open our hearts to repentance and correction.

God answers prayer. I have seen Him do it in my life, and I've seen Him do it in the lives of others. "If my people who are called by my name humble themselves, and pray and seek my face and turn from their wicked ways, then I will hear from heaven and will forgive their sin and heal their land" (2 Chronicles 7:14).

Look for clues about prayer in that verse: 1) pray with an attitude of humility, 2) seek God's face (what makes Him smile), and 3) turn from evil ways. God places a high value on those three elements.

If you struggle with broken patterns in your life, how should you pray? Start with humbly offering up David's prayer from Psalm 139... *Search me and know me, and see if there's any hurtful way in me.* God would love to answer that prayer, but you have to listen for His answer, and you need to respond in obedience. The Holy Spirit can speak in a quiet voice through Scripture, or He can use a table saw. Whatever it takes to get God's message through to His wayward sheep.

When we pray, we want instant results, but life doesn't work that way. Change occurs on a slow, day-to-day basis. In *Life's Healing Choices*, John Baker writes:

Ask God to help you just for today: "Lord, just for this day, I want to be patient and not get angry. Just for today, protect me from going to those Internet sites. Just for today, help me think pure thoughts instead of lustful ones. Just for today, I want to be positive instead of negative." Ask God to help you just for today, and take it a little bit at a time.[17]

LAMPPOST TWO: MEDITATE ON SCRIPTURE AND JOURNALING

The Bible consists of 66 books written by 40 authors over a period of about 2,000 years, and it has an over-arching theme. God is love. He wants you to know His love and the freedom found in obedience.

Meditating on God's Word and allowing the Holy Spirit to convict you will guide how you live. From

King David in Psalm 119 we read: *"How sweet your words taste to me; they are sweeter than honey. Your commandments give me understanding; no wonder I hate every false way of life. Your word is a lamp to guide my feet and a light for my path"* (Psalm 119:103-105 NLT). Over my lifetime, I could have saved myself so much pain if I had only honored God and His Word enough to *obey consistently.* A less painful way to move through life would be gaining understanding through God's Word and using it as a guide and light for our paths.

Here are three reasons for that:

First: *God's Word restrains sin.* Knowing God's expectations for your life, along with an obedient heart, will result in a godly life. The Holy Spirit works to teach you about your weaknesses through Scripture.

Second: *God's Word empowers you to minister to others.* Just as we should be open to other believers speaking into our lives, we should be willing to speak God's Word into others' lives.

Third: *God's Word is trustworthy.* God has communicated His desires and His guidance throughout the Bible. We would be fools if we ignored the power His Word wields, both for our lives and for the lives of those with whom we come into contact.

Journaling helps you meditate on God's work in your life. When you journal, you commemorate God's transformation of your heart. I admit, for years I mocked people who journaled…especially men who journaled. Now I'm one of those guys, and I feel strongly enough about that process to give it space here.

Journals serve to process and memorialize your thoughts and feelings, and most importantly, they help you remember how God works in you by His Holy Spirit. "Let this be written for a future generation, that a people not yet created may praise the LORD" (Psalm 102:18 NIV). Journals remind you how God uses your weaknesses.

When I look back though my journals, I see the faithful God who has led me, and who has kept His promises. Those journals testify to the truth of God's work in my life.

LAMPPOST THREE: ACCOUNTABILITY

Without confession, healing just doesn't happen: "Therefore, confess your sins to one another and pray for one another, that you may be healed" (James 5:16). *When unrighteous actions and habits snare you, the relationship you have with God weakens, and relationships here on Earth grow apart.* Seeking God's forgiveness goes a long way to relieving us of the weight of those actions and healing relationships with Him. Power lies in agreeing with God about our sin and sharing our story with another believer.

Ask a "safe" friend who follows Christ to coffee or a meal. Share your struggle and ask for a regular check-up with them. Remember David's lament: "When I kept quiet about my sin, my bones wasted away from crying all day long" (Psalm 32:3 NLV). Silence is bondage, and it keeps us in a life of hiding. Deitrich Bonhoeffer from his book *Life Together* wrote:

In the presence of another Christian I no longer need to pretend. In another Christian's presence I am permitted to be the sinner that I am...Other Christians stand before us as the sign of God's truth and grace. They have been given to us to help us.[18]

Our unconfessed broken ways stand in the way of our prayers. "If I had not confessed the sin in my heart, the Lord would not have listened. But God did listen! He paid attention to my prayer. Praise God, who did not ignore my prayer or withdraw his unfailing love from me" (Psalm 66:18-20 NLT).

In 1991, John Baker founded Celebrate Recovery at Saddleback Church in Lake Forest, California. Celebrate Recovery is a Christ-centered, 12-step recovery program for anyone struggling with hurt, pain, or addiction. A Celebrate Recovery gathering creates a safe space to find community and freedom from the issues that might be controlling one's life. From my experience in those meetings, people embrace confession, and they leave judgment at the door. You will be welcomed with open arms.

OUR UNCONFESSED BROKEN WAYS STAND IN THE WAY OF OUR PRAYERS.

Over 35,000 churches across the world host Celebrate Recovery groups. If you desire a safe place for confession and accountability, then you should look into Celebrate Recovery: CelebrateRecovery.com.

PUT OFF / RENEW / PUT ON

Those three lamps: prayer, meditation on God's Word, and accountability put spotlights where you are weak in obeying God's commands. They help in our transformation process. As new creations, cooperating with the Holy Spirit, we will see changes in our lives proving we have begun following the desires of God. With the Spirit of Christ living inside us, we will become uncomfortable with many of our past thoughts and actions that existed in the darkness of our lives. We should pray we come to hate the darkness we loved so much at one time. We need to voluntarily kill the sin we so desperately want to hide.

If we kill those wrong actions, our broken lives, which once pursued the darkness, will move toward the illumination the Bible provides. We don't do this perfectly...after all, like sheep, we're just trying to follow the Shepherd, but we do have an active role to play in this:

> Put off your old self, which belongs to your former manner of life and is corrupt through deceitful desires, and to be renewed in the spirit of your minds, and to put on the new self, created after the likeness of God in true righteousness and holiness (Ephesians 4:22-24).

CONTINUAL, GRADUAL, OBEDIENT TRANSFORMATION

With the Holy Spirit prompting us to change, we begin putting off disobedience, renewing our mind and putting on godly habits. This transformation happens by knowing God's Word and following the Holy Spirit through a number of steps.

If you cooperate with the Holy Spirit, you can:

- Change your thoughts

- Change your desires

- Change your actions

- Change your habits

When you do that, the Spirit of God will:

- Change your character, and

- Change your destiny

RENEWING YOUR THOUGHTS

We need to do all we can to transform our thoughts so our habits conform to Christ's desire for godliness. "Don't copy the behavior and customs of this world, but let God transform you into a new person by changing the way you think. Then you will learn to know God's will for you, which is good and pleasing and perfect" (Romans 12:2 NLT). What does it take to renew our minds?

A. WE NEED TO KNOW WHAT IS WRONG:

We need to do some deep self-examination. Pray King David's prayer to be searched from Psalm 139:23-24. We have already done exercises which helped you recognize your elephant sin. Let's start there. Elyse Fitzpatrick points out why we struggle with knowing our wrongs:

> Not only do we consciously choose to sin; we habitually do so. If it's your practice to lie when you're under pressure, then you'll find yourself doing it even when it's not a conscious choice. If you always eat chocolate when you're feeling sorry for yourself, then if there's chocolate around, and you're feeling badly, you'll go for it...It's the way we serve other gods without being aware of it.[19]

B. WE NEED TO KNOW WHAT TO OBEY:

If you don't know what God says about your brokenness, you need to find scriptures that speak to your weakness. In the Appendix of this book I have listed Bible verse that relate to a number of sin issues. Look up several to see if they fit your situation. Ask other believers for their insight. Remember, you have a job to do here. You are *Co-Operating* in this process. When you find scriptures that apply to your particular issue, memorize one or two key verses that speak to your situation.

C. WE NEED TO CONFESS WE HAVE SINNED AND ASK FOR CONVICTION:

Confession starts with godly sorrow. This is where humility comes into contact with your brokenness. If you want to leave your hiding place, your humility will lead you into confession of your sin. Ask for the Holy Spirit to convict you, and then act on His prompting.

D. WE NEED TO TAKE SWIFT ACTION ON OUR THOUGHT LIFE:

"We break down every thought and proud thing that puts itself up against the wisdom of God. We take hold of every thought and make it obey Christ" (2 Corinthians 10:5 NLV). Your fleshly thoughts tend to focus on that elephant sin, and you "coddle" those thoughts and the actions that follow. That coddling and wrongdoing is *what you need to put off.* You need to take hold of it and make it obey Christ through what you have discovered in the Bible. This requires you to take strong action on your thought life. You need to catch yourself early in this process and call yourself out.

You won't do this until you hate the sin in your life. Proverbs 8:13 tells us if we want to "honor" or "fear" the Lord, we need to hate evil, hate our wrongs. If you haven't reached a point of hating your rebellious actions, then you aren't honoring God with your life as He calls you to do.

E. WE NEED TO THINK DIFFERENT, GODLY THOUGHTS:

"Finally, brothers, whatever is true, whatever is honorable, whatever is just, whatever is pure, whatever is lovely, whatever is commendable, if there is any excellence, if there is anything worthy of praise, think about these things" (Philippians 4:8).

Again, John Baker writes:

> Did you know that there are more than seven thousand promises in the Bible? These promises are the perfect channel to change to…You can change your channel by learning to memorize Scripture…When they are in your mind, you can change the channel on any negative thoughts the enemy or others give you.[20]

When you catch yourself falling into your habit of coddling your elephant sin thoughts, you need to shift toward godly thinking. Satan loves a vacuum and will jump in with his suggestion that you deserve to hang on to that wrong habit. Don't let him do this. Make a list of those pure, lovely, commendable, excellent, praiseworthy things to think about. This is key to the practice of putting on godly behavior.

GODLY THOUGHTS LEAD TO GODLY DESIRES

Blue John Canyon held Aron Ralston as a prisoner for five days. Aron had to begin thinking differently about his situation before he decided to cut off his arm. After all, his hand began to decay, and would no longer be of any use to him. If he wanted to live, he had to sacrifice his hand. He had to rethink the value of his hand versus the value of living.

You need to change your thoughts as well. If the Holy Spirit has convicted you of wrongdoing, and your thoughts begin to change, you have crossed the first hurdle. Your desires will begin to change because you think differently.

BUT WHEN YOUR THOUGHT LIFE BEGINS TO CHANGE, YOUR DESIRES WILL FOLLOW THOSE GODLY THOUGHTS, AND YOUR WORSHIP LIFE WILL BE CORRECTED.

In the past your ungodly thoughts led you to ungodly desires and you created functional idols, just like I did with alcohol. But when your thought life begins to change, your desires will follow those godly thoughts, and your worship life will be corrected. You will begin to worship God with your whole life instead of worshipping your fleshly desires.

The Apostle Paul wrote about this in Galatians 5:16: "But I say, walk by the Spirit, and you will not gratify the desires of the flesh." Only when you cooperate with the Holy Spirit will you be able to correct your worship and your desires.

Godly Desires Lead to Godly Actions

We act on our desires, for good or for bad. If we desire God above all else, our actions will reveal that. If we act to fulfill our fleshly desires, those actions will result in what we want to hide. "A good man produces good deeds from a good heart. And an evil man produces evil deeds from his hidden wickedness. Whatever is in the heart overflows into speech" (Luke 6:45 TLB).

At this point, you begin to "put on" your new nature. Your new, redeemed self begins to form, and there will be "fruit" in that—godly fruit.

Continual Godly Actions Create Godly Habits

The book of Galatians talks about the "fruits of the Spirit." "But the fruit of the Spirit is love, joy, peace, patience, kindness, goodness, faithfulness, gentleness, self-control" (Galatians 5:22-23a). We see evidence of the work of the Spirit of Christ in our lives.

When you act on godly desires, you will develop godly habits that can last a lifetime. When your godly actions turn into habits, they would be called "fruits of the Spirit." When you are hiding, good fruit ceases to form in your life, and you are not serving in God's Kingdom as He would desire. We can see how changing our thoughts, desires, and actions enable us to step into serving our Lord.

Godly Habits Change Our Character

As you change your patterns and habits, you will see changes in your character. You begin to exhibit some of the "fruits of the Spirit" mentioned in Galatians 5. Godly actions/habits become the foundation for your new godly character. This process moves slowly, but with the help of the Holy Spirit and your accountability partners, you have God's assurance your life will change dramatically.

GODLY CHARACTER CHANGES ONE'S DESTINY

All of the steps above form our destiny in life. That transformed destiny grows out of our initial thoughts. If a person desires to come out of hiding and change trajectory, the first change needs to take place in the mind, in renewing one's thoughts. Correction of one's pathway is possible but becomes more difficult later in life as habitual patterns become embedded.

When we renew our mind, setting our thoughts on the Spirit of God, we can be assured of a transformed life of freedom.

CHANGE IS IN OUR HANDS

A call to confession, repentance, and transformation shouts to all of us from the book of Matthew. There we see John the Baptist challenge the Pharisees with these words: "Do the things that show you really have changed your hearts and lives" (Matthew 3:8 NCV). Other versions of that verse translate it as: "Produce fruit, keeping with repentance." This verse calls us to partner with the Holy Spirit in renewing our mind, living out a new life pattern that pursues kingdom purpose.

WHEN WE RENEW OUR MIND, SETTING OUR THOUGHTS ON THE SPIRIT OF GOD, WE CAN BE ASSURED OF A TRANSFORMED LIFE OF FREEDOM.

That same call goes out to you today. The "fruit" John the Baptist spoke of are the good works God prepared just for you. That's your true purpose in life. Hiding isn't in your job description.

We need to be more intentional about our weaknesses. We cannot live as victims of our flesh. We have the ability to control the thoughts triggered by our flesh, or by the temptations of Satan. We also have access to both the Holy Spirit, and God's Word to deal with Satan's schemes. But we must discipline our lives by cooperating with the guidance of the Holy Spirit, and we also must accept the help of our community of faith.

God loves you no matter where you walk on the pathway toward Him. If you are walking away, He still looks forward to your return. He will graciously accept you into His refuge, but it's up to you to turn around.

Again: You're not alone.

Everyone has a hiding place.

Hope is in letting God's Light in.

For Discussion

1. Ephesians 4:22-24 talks about putting off wrongdoing, renewing one's mind, and putting on righteousness. Discuss what you think it means to "renew your mind." Is there a "standard" for a renewed mind? (Hint: Psalm 119:103-105, Galatians 5:22-23, and Philippians 4:8).

_____

_____

_____

_____

_____

_____

2. Read Ephesians 5:1-21 for "action items" (you will find at least 15). What are the actions believers are called to "put off" and what actions are believers called to "put on?"

_____

_____

_____

_____

_____

3. Jeremiah 17:9 paints a rather bleak picture of our hearts as deceitful and sick. Is it hypocritical for Paul to write believers are children of the light in Ephesians 5:8-9? How can both be true?

_____

_____

_____

_____

_____

_____

4. Paul writes about putting to death "the deeds of the body" in Romans 8:13. This makes it sound like serious business. On a scale of 1-10, how serious are you about killing the elephant sin in your life?

_____

_____

_____

_____

_____

5. Read 2 Corinthians 10:5. Share a time when you told the Holy Spirit you didn't want to take every thought captive and wanted to coddle your sin just a bit more? How do you think God feels about that? How does God's perspective make you feel?

_____

_____

_____

_____

_____

_____

CHAPTER 6

REFUGE

When you stray from His presence, He longs for you to come back. He weeps that you are missing out on His love, protection and provision. He throws His arms open, runs toward you, gathers you up, and welcomes you home.

Charles Stanley

IN LUKE 15, Jesus told three parables about lost coins, lost sheep, and a lost, wayward son. All of the parables center around the theme of God's love for lost people. The most famous of all Christ's parables, the story of the prodigal son, reveals so much we need to know about God's forgiveness. By the way, because we don't use the word "prodigal" often, I wanted to let you know it refers to a *wastefully extravagant person.*

To illustrate the point further, Jesus told them this story: A man had two sons. The younger son told his father, 'I want my share of your estate now before you die.' So his father agreed to divide his wealth between his sons.

A few days later this younger son packed all his belongings and moved to a distant land, and there he wasted all his money in wild living. About the time his money ran out, a great famine swept over the land, and he began to starve. He persuaded a local farmer to hire him, and the man sent him into his fields to feed the pigs. The young man became so hungry that even the pods he was feeding the pigs looked good to him. But no one gave him anything.

When he finally came to his senses, he said to himself, "At home even the hired servants have food enough to spare, and here I am dying of hunger! I will go home to my father and say, 'Father, I have sinned against both heaven and you, and I am no longer worthy of being called your son. Please take me on as a hired servant.'"

So he returned home to his father. And while he was still a long way off, his father saw him coming. Filled with love and compassion, he ran to his son, embraced him, and kissed him. His son said to him, "Father, I have sinned against both heaven and you, and I am no longer worthy of being called your son." But his father said to the servants, "Quick! Bring the finest robe in the house and put it on him. Get a ring for his finger and sandals for his feet. And kill the calf we have been fattening. We must celebrate with a feast, for this son of mine was dead and has now returned to life. He was lost, but now he is found." So the party began.

Meanwhile, the older son was in the fields working. When he returned home, he heard music and dancing in the house, and he asked one of the servants what was going on. "Your brother is back," he was told, "and your father has killed the fattened calf. We are celebrating because of his safe return." (Luke 15:11-27 NLT).

ALL ABOUT THE FATHER

Growing up, my Sunday School teachers often used a flannelgraph storyboard with little figures cut out of felt to teach Bible stories. At the time, I thought the message of this parable centered on a bad younger son who ran away from home, a good older son who worked hard, and a father who threw a party when the younger son finally came back home. The teachers encouraged us to "be good" like the older son, and not run away from home. Not until much later in my life did I see the true complexity of this story.

Our heavenly Father extravagantly loves His children. This parable illustrates the deep love God has for both the morally corrupt, as well as the prideful and self-righteous person. When Jesus told this story, He shared it with the "tax collectors and sinners," the outcasts of Jewish society, and the religious elite the "Pharisees and the scribes." Jesus presented this story to two groups that didn't want anything to do with each other.

The Pharisees and scribes thought poorly of the tax collectors and sinners, and they didn't want to become "unclean" by hanging out with this kind of person. Not surprisingly, the tax collectors and sinners felt judged by the Pharisees and scribes, and they felt unworthy to be around these religious elite.

Jesus felt comfortable with both groups. He loved them both, but He also saw the brokenness in the hearts of each group. Jesus told this story to let them know (along with us) that God seeks out and loves all sinners, and we should do the same. Jesus lived and loved this way, and in doing so, He gave us a vision of the heart of God.

THE REFUSAL OF REFUGE

Pride motivated the prodigal son to selfishly ask his father to give him his inheritance. As we've seen before, prideful passions form the core of the prodigal's eagerness to fulfill his lusts. The father has provided the younger son with safety and comfort, but this isn't enough to satisfy the young man. The request of the prodigal shows he has no respect for his father, or for the father's provision of safety, security, and daily needs. He only desires the father's material possessions. He wants to make his I Worship Me decisions regarding how he will benefit from his dad's stuff.

The prodigal son turns his back on the love of the father, but he also leaves behind the refuge of the family home. Just like many foolish people today, he makes a self-focused decision to pursue a life apart from the safety and security his father provided.

Just like the prodigal, we often walk away from our heavenly Father to go after the desires of our hearts. We pridefully assume those things will make us happy, but they don't. They might bring a temporary pleasure, but they can't bring true contentment.

CONTEXT IS CRUCIAL

The prodigal son story becomes so much more revealing about the heart of God when you see it in the context of Jesus's day. We overlook many important details because we fail to understand the parable in the way Jesus's audience heard it.

To begin with, the request of the younger son to receive his inheritance early would have been unthinkable in first-century Israel. In those times, the older son would have received twice as much inheritance as the younger son, and this would have occurred at the time of the death of their father. In this story, the younger son asks his father to give him one third of all of the father's assets, before the father's death. In essence, the younger son says to his father, "I don't care about you, father, I only value your money. I wish you were dead."

The father in the story has every right to not only deny the younger son's request, but also to severely discipline the boy for making such a request. Jesus could not have told a more extreme example of a shameful and self-focused individual than the younger son.

The prodigal's request dishonors his family, and for the father to grant the request would have been seen as a shameful act on the father's part. And yet the father gives into the desires of his son, knowing his son will likely squander the money he's given. Christ told the story this way to reveal the grace of our heavenly Father who gives all of us what we don't deserve.

CHRIST TOLD THE STORY THIS WAY TO REVEAL THE GRACE OF OUR HEAVENLY FATHER WHO GIVES ALL OF US WHAT WE DON'T DESERVE.

Here we can see God's commitment to allowing His children to exercise free will. Some might argue it would be unloving for a father to allow his son to waste his inheritance without restraint. He rarely intervenes to stop people from pursuing their wrongdoing.

THE RUSH TO SATISFY SELF

After he receives his inheritance, the prodigal son has a fire sale to liquidate all of his newly acquired assets. Those assets would be land his father owned as well as livestock. In just a few days, he turns it all into cash. And why not…it's hard to be a free-wheeling teenager when you're trying to herd a bunch of sheep.

The prodigal hurries to get away from his father's home and pursue the immoral life he envisions. He chooses to go to a distant land to run after wine, women, and song. For some reason, I don't remember any flannelgraph figures of prostitutes. Jesus tells us it was "a distant land." *For the prodigal, a distant place is a good hiding place.*

In this far-away land the young man lives up to his name by extravagantly wasting all of the inheritance his father graciously granted him. In that distant location, he worships his comfort idols and builds a hiding place for those sin-filled exploits. But he runs out of money, and a famine strikes the land.

REALITY BITES, HUMILITY FOLLOWS

When the famine hits, the prodigal becomes an indentured servant to a Gentile farmer, feeding pigs. I'm sure when Jesus told this part of the story, his audience turned up their noses and collectively said, "Ugh, that's gross!" For Jews, this would have been the lowest of lowly positions. In first century Jerusalem, shepherds got a bad rap, but people who fed pigs would have been lower than shepherds. God had commanded the Jews to avoid pigs at all costs.

HAVE YOU MADE CHOICES IN YOUR LIFE WHICH THAT HAVE TAKEN YOU FAR AWAY FROM A SAFE AND LOVING PLACE?

The prodigal son had a long time to think about his life on the way down to the bottom, to the mud pit. There he "came to his senses." Isn't it interesting how it takes reaching the bottom of life to wake up to the truth…to reality…to humility?

Have you made choices in your life that have taken you far away from a safe and loving place? If so, this parable offers great news of redemption and renewal giving you hope for your story.

TRUST AND FEAR

Maybe the smell of pig dung or the severe hunger pains caused the prodigal son to come to his senses. Whatever it was, he decides to leave his destitute hiding place. He begins to appreciate what he left behind. He remembers the generosity of his father whose hired servants have more than enough food to eat. The prodigal finally sees his father had been a loving and trustworthy man, and he wants to return to that safe place…that refuge. In remembering his father's love, the prodigal is able to overcome his fear and shame. He repents and decides he wants to again live in the safety his father is known to provide.

The trust of his father's love and kindness turns the prodigal toward home, and toward refuge and sanctuary. As he turns toward home, he fears the shame of answering for his impetuous decision to run away and for the squandering of his inheritance. The level of shaming he faces will be intense, and he expects he will have to work for years to regain any of his previous position in the family.

The prodigal practices a humble speech he will deliver when he sees his father. He acknowledges his unworthiness to be called a son in his father's household, and hopes that possibly, his father will consider hiring him as a servant.

Just like this young man, we have all rebelled against God, and we are unworthy of His love and forgiveness. But just like the prodigal, we can trust the Father's love.

WHAT LOVE IS THIS?

As the boy approaches his hometown, his father sees him from a long way off. Just like our God, the father has been on the lookout for his son, hoping to see his return. Our Heavenly Father seeks after His lost children, and this parable illustrates this truth so beautifully. Because God loves us, He hates the sin which causes our distance from Him, and He wants us to come back home to His refuge and care.

When the father sees his son on the road home, he is filled with loving compassion, and in his desire to greet the son, he runs toward him. In that culture, for a nobleman to run through his village would have been a shameful act. Noblemen don't run, servants run. In the Middle East at that time, for a nobleman to show his legs was shameful, but the father in Jesus's story didn't care. He willingly bore the shame because he loves his child so much, and his eagerness to greet the son drives him to run.

Not only does the father shamefully run through the town, but he also embraces his son and kisses him. Wow...hugging and kissing a boy who has been slopping pigs? Jesus's audience would have let out another groan of "Ewwww," and would have called Jesus's parable far-fetched. But God's grace and love are just that—far-fetched.

From a distance, the father senses the repentant heart of his son. I would imagine the son's body language telegraphs his humble heart and his shame. The son blurts out his confession, but the father doesn't need the words...he sees through them to the contrite heart which lies beneath.

Where Is the Father's Shame?

Let's take a break. Go back and look at the prodigal's story at the beginning of this chapter for just a moment. Look through everything describing the prodigal's father, and all the words he says. Underline everything you see as a shaming attitude by the father.

How many incidents of shaming did you find? None?

Could this be a horrible mistake in Jesus's storytelling, or can we learn something here?

The prodigal's father shows himself to be "filled with love and compassion." The father ignores any words that might shame, but he calls for the village to celebrate his son's return. There's a lesson here. Jesus told the story precisely to make a point. Neither Jesus nor His Father initiate shame. This isn't in God's character. His char-

NEITHER JESUS NOR HIS FATHER INITIATE SHAME. THIS ISN'T IN GOD'S CHARACTER.

acter exhibits love, compassion, grace, mercy, and an overwhelming desire to cover shame.

The prodigal's father had every right to punish his son and to shun him, or at least to make him "work his way back into the family." But that's not the heart of the father. Mercy and grace live in the heart of the father toward his wayward son. He didn't give his son what the prodigal deserved, but instead he gave the son what he didn't deserve.

The Covering of Shame

When the son appears on the horizon, the father's love motivates him to rush toward his lost son for another reason. Perhaps he wants to protect his son from the shame cast by the villagers.

To protect his son from shame, the father demands his servants immediately get his finest robe, along with a ring and sandals. Jesus's audience knew the significance and symbolism of these three items. Everyone would have known the implication Christ intended, and it would have been shocking to them because it rubs against the grain of their culture.

The father's finest robe is only worn at the biggest and best celebrations. Instead of being worried about the filth of his son, the father concerns himself with honoring the son's return with a celebration. The robe he offers will cover the son's shameful, ragged clothing that smelled like a pigpen.

INSTEAD OF BEING WORRIED ABOUT THE FILTH OF HIS SON, THE FATHER CONCERNS HIMSELF WITH HONORING THE SON'S RETURN WITH A CELEBRATION.

Here's a review question for you: Where have we seen this kind of act on God's part before? Yup, you're right: *God made clothes out of animal skins to cover the shame of Adam and Eve.* This isn't a coincidence, folks! This is the reality of God's character.

The ring the father asks to be given to his youngest would be a signet ring bearing the mark of the family. In giving this ring to the prodigal, the father proclaims: "All I have is yours." Slaves and hired servants went barefoot in those days and didn't wear sandals. In asking the servants to get sandals for his son, the father makes the statement he accepts the young man back as a member of the household, and not a servant.

The prodigal's father makes a preemptive strike against the shame that might be coming the boy's way. Not only did he physically cover the prodigal's shame with a robe, a ring, and sandals, but he calls for a party and the slaughtering of the family's fatted calf. The entire village welcomes the son "back from the dead."

THE UGLIEST ACT OF LOVE

Symbolism exudes from the story of the prodigal son, and we see the entire gospel of Jesus. Jesus tells a masterful story, painting a picture of how God, our heavenly Father, loves us, and how His love casts out our fear of condemnation…if we turn toward Him and accept His love. The father of the prodigal son exhibits so many of the loving and forgiving characteristics of God.

Jesus's sacrifice of Himself on the cross must be the ugliest but most beautiful act of love this world has witnessed. God, through Christ's death, covers all our wrongs. He covers our sin by His love, just like the animal skins He crafted to cover the nakedness of Adam and Eve, and the finest robe the prodigal's father drapes over his filthy son.

JESUS'S SACRIFICE OF HIMSELF ON THE CROSS MUST BE THE UGLIEST BUT MOST BEAUTIFUL ACT OF LOVE THIS WORLD HAS WITNESSED.

Jesus's death and His resurrection take the eternal burden of all of our brokenness from our shoulders, and we can have great confidence in that. Our disobedience causes us to feel guilt and shame, but when Christ took our sin onto His crucified shoulders, He covered all of our wrongs, just as the prodigal's father did.

Roman soldiers fully stripped Christ naked and hung Him on a cross until He died. The writer of Hebrews tells us Christ despised the shame of the cross (Hebrews 12:2). *Not only did Jesus disregard the shame He bore personally, but He disregarded the shame He bore on our behalf.* Because Christ did that for us, we no longer have to bear the penalty or the shame of sin.

FORGIVENESS, FOREVER

This parable of the prodigal tells about a celebration hosted by the father upon the return of his son. Here Jesus points to the celebration going on right now in heaven. But the celebration isn't all about us. Yes, forgiveness covers our wrongs, and heavenly beings celebrate our return, but the celebration honors a forgiving and grace-filled God who invites fallen people to join His family and His banquet. *The father in this story also behaves as a prodigal…he is extravagantly wasteful in his love and kindness.*

Because of the sacrificial death of Jesus, His forgiveness covers our transgressions forever. Unlike a human who may bring up another person's wrongs at a future date, when God forgives, it's done, finished, forever:

> There is no God like you. You forgive those who are guilty of sin; you don't look at the sins of your people who are left alive. You will not stay angry forever, because you enjoy being kind. You will have mercy on us again; you will conquer our sins. You will throw away all our sins into the deepest part of the sea (Micah 7:18-19 NCV).

Timothy Keller reflects on the forgiveness of our Heavenly Father: "God's love and forgiveness can pardon and restore any and every kind of sin or wrongdoing. It doesn't matter who you are or what you've done…There is no evil the Father's love cannot pardon and cover, there is no sin that is a match for His grace."[21]

But Where's the Older Brother?

Someone is missing from the story here. Where is the older brother? The party begins, and the father doesn't send a servant out to the fields to share the good news of the prodigal's return with the older brother. How curious.

We will pick up the story of the older brother in the next chapter. Jesus crafted a second punchline to His story of the prodigal, and it's a message for all of us.

Coming to Your Senses

So many of us don't know this loving God we see in the story of the prodigal. He's the God whose eyes scan the horizon, searching for us, waiting for us. Somehow, we missed the memo along the way about Him being a forgiving Father, eager to cover our shame, to love us back into His family, into His refuge. We don't see Him for the God He is—a trustworthy comforter, a loving forgiver of sins, and a celebrator of returning lost souls. And He does all this with no shame in His voice. God offers grace and mercy to all who turn toward Him.

SO MANY OF US DON'T KNOW THIS LOVING GOD WE SEE IN THE STORY OF THE PRODIGAL.

In the parable of the prodigal, we don't see the father going out to hunt down his son and yank him out of the bed of a whore. God won't grab you by the neck as you feast your eyes on porn, and He won't drag you out of a bar, or clamp your mouth shut for gossiping.

But make note, the pivot point of this parable occurs when the prodigal son "came to his senses." If the prodigal hadn't done that, then there would not have been a happy ending. The father would not have seen his son coming down the dusty pathway back to his waiting arms and his refuge.

When the prodigal reaches the end of his rope and considers the true character of his father, he decides to trust in his father's love and kindness. He remembers how his father had treated the hired men, and he realizes it would be safe to return home to his father's refuge. Trusting in love gives confidence in repentance.

Just as the prodigal came to his senses, maybe you're a person who needs to "come to your right mind." You need to make a decision to partner with God to begin your return to His refuge. You begin this process by humbly allowing God's redemptive light to shine into your dark place. It's scary, I know, and you're afraid of what might happen next. But many people will testify it is so worth it.

FREEDOM IN THE FATHER'S REFUGE

If you, like the prodigal son, have run from God, and have started to build a place to hide, you have a decision to make. You can remain in your solitary hiding place separated from God and others, or you can come to your senses and trust in a loving God who wants to welcome you back home with loving arms, a fine robe, and a party.

IF YOU, LIKE THE PRODIGAL SON, HAVE RUN FROM GOD, AND HAVE STARTED TO BUILD A PLACE TO HIDE, YOU HAVE A DECISION TO MAKE.

Why would Jesus make such a point of telling us that the prodigal's father planned a celebration for the entire village? There must be something for us to learn here. All three of the parables from Luke 15 refer to a celebration over valuable lost things, animals, and people. Can we take a clue from Jesus that lost sinners should be celebrated when they confess, repent, and return?

Jesus's story about the prodigal and his father paints such a clear picture of His love for all of us. This one parable distills the truth of God's grace and mercy and serves to remind us all: *In the Father's refuge are great joy, freedom, and celebration.*

For Discussion

1. Luke 15 contains 3 stories of things, animals, or people who were lost. Is there a story you might share about a time you were lost because of decisions you made? What made you "come to your senses"?

_____

_____

_____

_____

_____

_____

2. Do you see God (Father, Son, and Spirit) as being safe or do you see Him as dangerous? How does your vision of God compare to how Jesus portrayed God in the story of the prodigal?

_____

_____

_____

_____

_____

3. Read Micah 7:19. We are told that God casts ALL our sins into the depths of the sea. Share why that might be hard for you to understand.

_____

_____

_____

_____

_____

_____

CHAPTER 7

WE HAD TO CELEBRATE

You plead my cause, You right my wrongs.
You break my chains, You overcome.
You gave Your life to give me mine.
You say that I am free.
How can it be.
How can it be.

Lauren Daigle

W E LEFT THE prodigal parable with the father hosting the village in a celebration of the return of his son. A joy-filled banquet begins with fresh meat roasting over a fire. But out in the courtyard we hear harsh words exchanged, and anger rises.

The older son returns from the field, only to find there's a party going on for his wayward brother. He refuses to join the party, because he's not at all happy his younger brother has come home. The father pleads with the older brother to join in the celebration, but the elder son responds rudely:

The older brother was angry and wouldn't go in. His father came out and begged him, but he replied, "All these years I've slaved for you and never once refused to do a single thing you told me to. And in all that time you never gave me even one young goat for a feast with my friends. Yet when this son of yours comes back after squandering your money on prostitutes, you celebrate by killing the fattened calf!" (Luke 15:28-30 NLT).

Another Self-Focused Heart

The elder son feels slighted, and he throws a little hissy fit. We

can almost hear him whining about slaving away for years and years and getting nothing in return. He's ticked off because his father has slaughtered the fatted calf for his brother. Some writers think that the calf was being fattened up for the older brother's wedding.

He probably feels his younger brother should be harshly disciplined, or there should be some kind of penance for his wrongdoing. Either way, he reveals his true heart. There is no appreciation for the forgiving, grace-filled heart of his father. We see that just like the prodigal son, this brother shows his hidden agenda: coveting his father's assets. He takes his father's love for granted, and presumes that since the prodigal left home, he deserves to be the only one worthy of receiving the father's blessing.

The first-born son and his younger sibling are both blessed by the loving, gracious heart of the father, and the elder brother misses this point entirely. The father welcomes both sons into the safety, comfort, and refuge he offers.

No grace exists in the heart of the older son for either his father or his brother. He doesn't share his father's loving character for the lost. He divides life into "worthy" and "unworthy." This brother sees himself as the only one worthy and his younger brother is not.

WE HAD TO CELEBRATE

In chapter 15 of Luke's Gospel, Jesus tells three stories that show His heart, and by extension, the heart of God. In Luke 15:4-7, there's the parable of the lost sheep, and it ends with these words: "In the same way, there is more joy in heaven over one lost sinner who repents and returns to God than over ninety-nine others who are righteous and haven't strayed away!" Jesus follows up with a story about a precious coin that is lost but then found. The last verse of the parable says: "In the same way, there is joy in the presence of God's angels when even one sinner repents."

Just in case some in Jesus's audience missed the clues, He told one last story of the prodigal, and He ends with the same message delivered to the older brother:

> His father said to him, "Look, dear son, you have always stayed by me, and everything I have is yours. We had to celebrate this happy day. For your brother was dead and has come back to life! He was lost, but now he is found!" (Luke 15:31-32 NLT).

We had to celebrate. The brother who we thought was dead has come back to life. He was lost, and now he is back with us.

Jesus builds His story line up to this point. Heaven rejoices over just one sinner repenting, and heavenly voices celebrate more at the return of one sinner than 99 who have followed righteous living. Three times, we are told of the heart of God for lost souls. God looks for and longs for the return of His lost sheep, His children, you and me.

THE GRACIOUS FORGIVENESS GOD OFFERS IN WELCOMING THE SINNER HOME IS THE PRIMARY REASON TO CELEBRATE.

These three stories tell about the joy shared by God, Christ, and all the heavenly beings over a repentant person. An expression of great joy rises when people stop hiding their brokenness, and they turn their lives back toward God. The gracious forgiveness God offers in welcoming the sinner home is the primary reason to celebrate.

ABRUPT ENDING TO THE STORY

Jesus didn't tie the prodigal's story up with a nice pretty bow. He just left us wondering what happens next. Did the older brother join in the celebration? Did he stomp away in anger?

When Jesus finished his parables, both the tax collectors and sinners in the audience, as well as the Pharisees and the scribes, had something to ponder. Jesus delivers multiple messages packed into this one parable. First and foremost, He has a message for everyone about grace, love, and unity in the family of God. Second, He addresses the foolish behavior of the people who ignore following God's moral commands and who run after their worldly desires. And last, He speaks to the heart of the legalistic Pharisees and scribes who invest more time and energy on their self-imposed rules than in loving others and seeking the lost.

The 'Sinners'

Jesus wanted the "tax collectors and sinners" to see themselves in the life of the wayward prodigal who turned his back on righteous living to pursue his path of hedonistic, self-focused exploits. These were people who lived on the fringes of society, but nevertheless, Jesus welcomed them into a relationship.

These people felt the guilt and shame of their lives on a daily basis (due in part to the judgmental Pharisees), but the message they heard that day whispered love, grace, and freedom in their ears. Jesus clearly taught that God wanted them to feel valued and welcome in His kingdom. Jesus pictured a God who seeks them out and desires their repentance, their return to His refuge.

JESUS'S MESSAGE FOR YOU IS THAT IT'S NOT TOO LATE TO RETURN TO HIS FAMILY.

In some way, maybe you can relate to the prodigal and those who have turned away from the path toward God's Light. Jesus's message for you is that it's not too late to return to His family. He is gracious, forgiving, and will welcome you back.

The Other Sinners

When Jesus talked about the older son in Luke 15, the Pharisees and scribes who were listening could relate to the son's angry response. They felt the same way about the manner in which the father welcomed his youngest back home.

The Pharisees and the scribes were addicted to rules. Not only did they work hard to follow the Ten Commandments, but beyond that, they tried to follow a whole bunch of other rules they had added to God's law. And they expected all the other devout Jews should do the same. They took great pride in how well they obeyed the law.

Some of the harshest words of Jesus Christ that are recorded in the New Testament are aimed at the Pharisees and the religious elite. He called them fools, blind guides, whitewashed tombs, and vipers. Why did He do this? *Jesus hated the pride, and the piousness of hypocritical religious leaders.* Jesus focused on loving God and loving others. When the Pharisees set themselves apart from others who seemed "unclean," they refused to model the humble, loving heart of Christ reaching out to others who are different.

JUST AS THE FATHER OFFERED GRACE AND LOVE TO BOTH OF HIS SONS, JESUS OFFERS GRACE AND LOVE TO ALL SINNERS WHO TURN TO HIM.

The parable of the prodigal draws a line in the sand for these religious elite. Jesus makes it clear they don't share God's open heart for all who repent. Their pride stood in the way of welcoming the outcasts. Jesus's message to these smug sinners is they are broken and in need of a savior. They need to recognize that in the big picture, no difference exists between them and the tax collectors and other sinners. Just as the father offered grace and love to both of his sons, Jesus offers grace and love to all sinners who turn to Him.

YOUR SON...YOUR BROTHER

Throughout these parables, Jesus makes a point of calling attention to the heart of God for the lost, and He teaches all of us how we should model the heart of our Heavenly Father. If this were not the case, then Jesus wasted a whole lot of words talking about celebrating the return of lost things/people. Jesus calls all of us to do a better job of seeking out the lost and celebrating transformed lives.

I want to draw your attention to a detail you might have missed in how Jesus taught this parable. In Luke 15:30, the older son refers to the prodigal as *"this son of yours."* He refuses to acknowledge his relationship to his brother. The older brother didn't want to have anything to do with his brother, and in many ways, he pushed himself away from his father too. He didn't share the father's love for everyone in the family.

But his father has a whole other way of looking at this. If you look at Luke 15:32, the father calls the prodigal *"your brother."* He reminds his elder son that *all three of them are part of one family.* Jesus designed His message for this specific audience, and for all of us as well.

WE HAVE MET THE ENEMY AND HE IS US

Pride and "righteousness" are strange bedfellows. Jesus portrays the older brother (and the Pharisees) as self-righteous and prideful, without a heart of compassion for the lost brother. Let's be honest. Sometimes we don't share our Father's heart for lost people.

LET'S BE HONEST. SOMETIMES WE DON'T SHARE OUR FATHER'S HEART FOR LOST PEOPLE.

Our Father in Heaven cares about the "least of these." And we are guilty (like the older brother) of not sharing our Heavenly Father's love and generosity. *That's because we care more about ourselves (and about "rules") than we care about glorifying God and loving others.*

God still hates pridefulness and piety. Here's what Dietrich Bonhoeffer wrote of a pious church.

The pious community permits no one to be a sinner. Hence all have to conceal their sins from themselves and from the community. We are not allowed to be sinners. Many Christians would be unimaginably horrified if a real sinner were suddenly to turn up among the pious. So we remain alone with our sin, trapped in lies and hypocrisy, for we are in fact sinners.[22]

"Alone with our sin, trapped in lies and hypocrisy." This sounds like a darkened hiding place, wouldn't you agree? Even those who come across as "righteous" can be hiding wrongs. Cloaking oneself with pious righteousness glosses over lies and hypocrisy.

LEVEL GROUND

You might have heard it said, "The ground is level at the foot of the cross." In case you haven't, here's what that means: We all disobey God, and from His viewpoint, no difference exists in any of us. One factor separates us from each other. Some of us have accepted Jesus as our Savior and made Him the Lord of our life, and others haven't. Those who have made Christ their Lord will join Him in heaven, whether they were tax collectors or Pharisees.

WE LIVE AS BROTHERS AND SISTERS WHO MESS UP AND NEED GOD'S FORGIVING GRACE AND MERCY.

We live as brothers and sisters who mess up and need God's forgiving grace and mercy. Whatever our sin might be, we owe our eternal life to one thing, the shed blood of Jesus.

WILL WE EXTEND THE SAME GRACE WE'VE RECEIVED?

The older brother had little love for the prodigal brother, and he showed no grace. He was too occupied with justifying himself in the eyes of his father and getting his own share of the father's wealth. He missed the clues of his father's loving heart, and he did nothing to mirror that love.

If the elder son wanted to please his father, and make him smile, he would have come home, washed up, put on his best clothes and best smile, and joined in on the celebration. But he didn't. He pouted, displeasing his father and disrespecting his brother. Fairness and following rules grabbed his heart, and he did this at the expense of loving his family.

WHO WILL WE LOVE?

Jesus made it clear what our priorities should be in Mark 12:30-31. When asked what the greatest commandment was, He responded with these words:

> "And you shall love the Lord your God with all your heart and with all your soul and with all your mind and with all your strength. The second is this: 'You shall love your neighbor as yourself.' There is no other commandment greater than these." (Mark 12:30-31).

The older brother didn't do either of these. He didn't love his father well, and he didn't love his younger sibling either.

Jesus modeled how we should love God and love others. Christ obeyed His Heavenly Father during His time here on Earth, He loved the marginalized sinner, and He laid down His life to satisfy

God's righteous anger over our unrighteous behavior. He showed us how to love well.

Will we follow His example? Will we love God as well as others who we pridefully think are not deserving of our love? Will we push them away, and in the process be poor ambassadors for Christ? I hope not.

More Celebration

In his anger and his pouting, the older brother missed the point of the celebration that day. Yes, his brother had returned, but the village celebrated *how he was welcomed home*. Without the forgiving heart of their father who ran to the prodigal, cov-

ering his shame, there would be nothing to celebrate. Max Lucado writes: "The difference between mercy and grace? Mercy gave the prodigal son a second chance. Grace gave him a feast."[23]

WILL WE FOLLOW HIS EXAMPLE? WILL WE LOVE GOD AS WELL AS OTHERS WHO WE PRIDEFULLY THINK ARE NOT DESERVING OF OUR LOVE?

That grace is the work of our Heavenly Father, and Jesus set an example for us in this parable of how we should celebrate both God's forgiveness of our sins, as well as the sinner who comes out of hiding. All of us need to celebrate our forgiveness. In turning toward home, the prodigal son found the freedom to celebrate in his story, and in his father's love. He lived to see refuge again, and he rejoiced in his forgiveness. His older brother didn't realize his need for forgiveness, and so the story ends in the tension between a grace-filled father and a pouting, pride-filled son.

Whether your life is represented by the pious older brother or the prodigal son, our Heavenly Father looks for your return. His refuge welcomes you into the safe place you so deeply want, and it's available to you right now. God's forgiveness of our sin gives rise to great joy and celebration.

For Discussion

1. Each of the parables in Luke 15 included celebrations. What does it say to you that Jesus intentionally included these celebrations? Do you think that hints at something else in the future?

_____

_____

_____

_____

_____

2. When it comes to celebrating sinners who have returned from being lost, do you see yourself more often in the shoes of the prodigal's father, or the older brother?

_____

_____

_____

_____

_____

3. Are you convicted by the term "pious"? Share why that might be.

_____

_____

_____

_____

_____

_____

4. Share about a time when you felt judged by an "older brother" type of person. How did it make you feel? Was it another Christian? How do you think it reflected on Christ?

_____

_____

_____

_____

_____

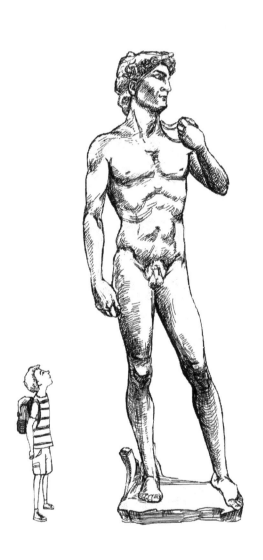

CHAPTER 8

JOY IN FORGIVENESS

But if we confess our sins, He will forgive our sins, because
we can trust God to do what is right. He will cleanse
us from all the wrongs we have done.

1 John 1:9 NCV

I GOT TO meet one of my heroes face-to-face in 1963. Well, not exactly face-to-face, since Michelangelo's statue of David in Florence, Italy stands about 17 feet tall, and that would have been a good 12 feet taller than me at that time.

Michelangelo began creating one of the world's most recognized works of art at 26. He spent three years completing the statue, and my dad joked if Michelangelo would have had another year, he might have put some clothes on David.

Michelangelo's statue memorializes one of the most famous stories from the Old Testament of the future king of Israel, the shepherd boy David killing the giant Goliath. That incident stands as one of two defining moments in David's life. You don't see the other incident in Sunday School flannelgraphs, the story of David's relationship with Bathsheba.

Testimonies of a King

If I had the ability to write Academy Award scripts, I don't think I could have created a better story than David and Bathsheba to illustrate the concept behind *Why We Hide*. All the juicy plot points are here: lustful coveting of a man's wife, adultery in the king's palace, attempts to conceal the shame of an illicit pregnancy, the murder of the woman's husband, the revelation of a King's sin, and then, the judgment of God. Stories don't get much richer in drama than that.

The prophet Samuel gave great detail to much of the narrative, and then we have David's words to fill us in on his deep emotions of guilt, shame, and regret. Three of David's psalms allow us to pull back the curtain of his life to understand how an adulterous murderer who chose a radical path to hide his wrongs could be called a "man after God's own heart."

Psalm 139—The Praising King

Too young to be serving in the Israelite army, David works as a shepherd for his father out in the countryside, guiding the sheep  and protecting them. Recently, he has been shuttling supplies to several of his soldier brothers stationed on the front lines of the battlefield where the army of Israel has engaged the Philistines.

As a shepherd, David has had a lot of experience fending off predators that might come after his father's sheep, and he has killed lions and bears that attacked the sheep. He developed great prowess using his sling to defend those sheep, and that skill will soon launch him into the Jewish national spotlight in 1010 BC.

Righteous Indignation

Neither the Israelite nor the Philistine armies want to aggressively engage, but every day, for 40 days, a Philistine giant named Goliath has stepped out of his camp on the south side of the valley, taunting the Israelite army and mocking their God. The Bible says Goliath was almost 10 feet tall, and *just his armor* weighed over 125 pounds.

One day, as David brought food to his brothers, he hears Goliath's challenge, and sees the fear the giant strikes in the Israelite army. David's immediate reaction is righteous anger and a desire to see someone deal with this man who casts insults at Israel and their God…his God. "For who is this uncircumcised Philistine, that he should defy the armies of the living God?" (1 Samuel 17:6).

Let's listen in as David testifies to his faith in God and God's power to deal with Goliath through his skills:

> Then David said to the Philistine, "You come to me with a sword and with a spear and with a javelin, but I come to you in the name of the Lord of hosts, the God of the armies of Israel, whom you have defied. This day the Lord will deliver you into my hand, and I will strike you down and cut off your head. And I will give the dead bodies of the host of the Philistines this day to the birds of the air and to the wild beasts of the earth, that all the earth may know that there is a God in Israel, and that all this assembly may know that the Lord saves not with sword and spear. For the battle is the Lord's, and He will give you into our hand"(1 Samuel 17:45-47).

Just as David predicted, he uses his sling to hurl a rock right into Goliath's forehead, killing him immediately. The Philistines freak out and begin to run away as the now-emboldened Israelite army roars their approval of David's courage.

National Hero

Overnight, David becomes a national hero in Israel. King Saul's

military leadership gives David command of 1,000 fighting men, though he's just a young teenager! God makes a covenant with David that His kingdom will live forever through the lineage of David (this points to Jesus Christ as a descendent of David), and David becomes king of Israel.

Scholars think David wrote Psalm 139 after God established this "Davidic Covenant." In this Psalm, we see David offering great honor to the worthiness of God:

> 1-2 "O Lord, you have searched me and known me! You know when I sit down and when I rise up; you discern my thoughts from afar.
>
> 4 Even before a word is on my tongue, behold, O Lord, you know it altogether.
>
> 7 Where shall I go from your Spirit? Or where shall I flee from your presence?
>
> 23-24 Search me, O God, and know my heart! Try me and know my thoughts! And see if there be any grievous way in me, and lead me in the way everlasting!" (Psalm 139, misc. verses).

David desires absolute purity in his commitment to serving God. David invites God to search him, to test him, and to purify him. But one problem emerged: David forgets this psalm. Just as we sometimes forget Who belongs on the throne of our lives, David did the same thing.

PSALM 51—THE BROKEN KING

No one talked about the next story in Sunday School because it's the story of David and Bathsheba. Just like the flannelgraph of the Prodigal Son, this story has elements that would be "R-rated."

At 50, David has seen his share of battles. While his troops fight the Ammonites, David strolls on the roof of his palace. As he gazes out over Jerusalem, something catches his eye.

PEEKING OVER FENCES

Okay, this is where the flannel board goes from a PG-13 rating to the R rating. We've got to put up the flannel-graph of the naked Bathsheba taking a bath on her patio. David couldn't resist the tempta-tion of her beauty. He sends a servant to fetch Bathsheba to bring her to his palace, and in time, she becomes pregnant.

Oh, and by the way, Bathsheba is married to Uriah the Hittite, one of David's "mighty fight-ing men." Uriah is on the battlefield, fighting the Ammonites, while the king messes around with his wife. Lovely!

Back to the flannelgraph. There's a baby bump starting to show now. David and Bathsheba have a problem. How do they cover up their little indiscretion—of the king of Israel getting the wife of one of his soldiers pregnant? Always the strategist, David comes up with a solution: Bring Uriah home from the war so he can sleep with his wife, and then it will look like Uriah fathered Bathsheba's baby. All of their immorality will be concealed. Brilliant!

An Arranged Murder

Uriah is a more loyal and dedicated soldier than David imagined. David encourages Uriah to take some time off and relax…go home, enjoy your wife…wink, wink. Uriah will have none of this kind of R&R. So David resorts to getting Uriah drunk, and still, Uriah holds out and refuses to be with Bathsheba.

Uriah's integrity causes David to take horrible steps to hide his sin. David sends a written message, delivered by Uriah himself, to his commander, Joab. The message instructs Joab to put Uriah in the heat of the battle, in harm's way, and then retreat from Uriah, leaving him exposed and helpless. Joab commands this to happen, and though Uriah dies by the sword of the Ammonites, in truth, his blood drips from David's hands.

How did that young, righteous, future king David go from a willingness to be intimately searched by God to hiding the evils of adultery and murder? He forgot. *He forgets the true King of both the universe, and his life. His lust, his pride, and his flesh cause him to turn away from his God, and put himself on the throne of his life.* David knows he should be saying I Worship God with his life, but he begins serving his fleshly desires.

We might be a bit more subtle in our wrongdoings, but just as capable as David.

Prophetic Punchline

With Uriah dead, David assumes all the ugly stuff he caused has been concealed and wrapped up with a pretty bow. Did he fool anyone by having Uriah killed? I doubt it. Did he fool God by trying to cover his unrighteousness? Certainly not.

The Lord sends the prophet Nathan to confront David, and he comes with a message from God. Nathan shares a story with David about a rich man needing to feed a visitor in his home. The rich man decides to steal the one and only lamb owned by a poor man. This lamb was raised as a pet, but the rich man has no concern for the poor man or his family, and he slaughters that lamb to feed his guest. What a great analogy pointing to the powerful King David taking the wife of one of his soldiers and sacrificing her for his pleasure.

When Nathan finishes the story, David's anger has him fum-ing, and he declares the rich man deserves to die. Nathan springs the trap he has laid for David. I can just picture Nathan, with a bony prophet finger, poking David in the chest and saying, "You are the man." I'm sure David is shocked as Nathan reveals the Lord knew everything David worked to cover up.

I SAW, I COVETED, I TOOK, I HID

Let's step away from David and Nathan for just a minute and look at a story from the book of Joshua. When Joshua fought the battle of Jericho, God instructed Israel to dedicate the entire spoils of the battle to Him. One soldier named Achan ignored God's command, and he keeps some of the spoils of the battle. He keeps a beautiful robe, a bunch of silver, and a bar of gold.

Achan's wrongdoing is found out, and when Joshua demands Achan confess, here's the conversation: "Then Joshua said to Achan, 'My son, give glory to the Lord God of Israel and give praise to Him. And tell me now what you have done; do not hide it from me.'" And Achan answered Joshua, "Truly I have sinned against the Lord God of Israel, and this is what I did: when I saw among the spoil a beautiful cloak from Shinar, and 200 shekels of silver, and a bar of gold weighing 50 shekels, then I coveted them and took them. And see, they are hidden in the earth inside my tent, with the silver underneath." (Joshua 7:19-21).

I want to point out the pattern Achan reveals, because this exposes the pattern of so much sin in our lives. *He says he saw, he coveted, he took, and he hid.* David followed the exact same path. He *saw* Bathsheba, he *coveted/wanted* her, and he *took* her to his bedroom. Then, when she becomes pregnant, he attempts to *hide* their wrongs, to the point he has Bathsheba's husband killed. Sin makes you stupid.

Sin has made me stupid as well. I have followed the exact same pattern in my life, and this is especially true in the situation of my aborted child. I saw, I coveted, I took for myself what wasn't mine, and then I concealed my immoral deeds by having my child killed. Guilty. I've made a lot of bad decisions in my life, but I haven't made a worse decision than that one. Thank God for His forgiveness.

In your life, could you point to a time of wanting something so much you sinned to get your desires, and then guilt and shame made you hide? God doesn't want you bound up in those emotions. He wants you to live the freedom that comes with confession and forgiveness.

I HAVE SINNED

David's invitation to be searched by God in Psalm 139 comes to pass. God saw David's numerous transgressions, and He uses Nathan to call him out. After Nathan reveals God's knowledge of the King's unrighteousness, a confession immediately comes from David's mouth. *"I have sinned against the Lord,"* he says. Nathan gives David reassurance that God forgives him, and he will not immediately die.

God knew David's heart broke over his wrongdoing, but all rebellion against God has ramifications. There will be significant consequences to David's outright scorning of the Lord. The child borne of the illicit affair with Bathsheba will die, and David's family will be torn apart by violence. Three of David's sons will die violent deaths.

Keeping one's wrongs secret can be debilitating. God wouldn't let David run from the weight of his sin, and David felt unbearable pressure. Hebrews 12:6 reminds us: discipline can be the most loving thing our heavenly Father (or a loving parent) can do. The purpose of God's discipline is to turn us back toward Him. If He didn't make attempts to turn us back toward Him, then He wouldn't be a loving Father, would He?

A Psalm of Confession

In Psalm 51, David is brutally honest in his repentance for his choices. David acknowledges his sin before God, and he desires cleansing and forgiveness. David wants God's mercy. In this psalm, David pleads with God for 20 actions, which include blotting out his sin, being washed, and being purged, and he asks God to hide

THE PURPOSE OF GOD'S DISCIPLINE IS TO TURN US BACK TOWARD HIM.

His face from his wrongs. He asks God to be allowed to hear joy and gladness again.

Verses in Psalm 51 might be familiar to you:

> Create in me a clean heart, O God, and renew a right spirit within me. Cast me not away from your presence, and take not your Holy Spirit from me. Restore to me the joy of your salvation, and uphold me with a willing spirit (Psalm 51:10-12).

> The sacrifices of God are a broken spirit; a broken and contrite heart, O God, you will not despise" (Psalm 51:17).

In Psalm 51:17 David hits the nail of confession on the head. *To break down the walls of our hiding place, we need a broken spirit. We need to become contrite and convicted by how we have missed the mark.*

PURPOSE IN PAIN

There can be a godly purpose in our wrongdoing. Remember, Romans 8:28-29 teaches us God can use all things to achieve His  goals. Perhaps we need to see that although sin results in collateral damage, it can and often does result in a "collateral blessing." In Psalm 51:12-13 we see David wants to bless others with his testimony: "Restore to me the joy of your salvation, and uphold me with a willing spirit. Then I will teach transgressors your ways, and sinners will return to you." This collateral blessing brings glory to God.

David wants to see a purpose in his brokenness. He cannot do anything to alter the sin he has committed. But David wants to caution others against unrighteousness, and he desires to proclaim the forgiveness of God.

PSALM 32—THE FORGIVEN KING

In Psalm 32, King David, the poet king, wrote a psalm of contrasts. He contrasts the crushing weight of secret sin with the freedom found in God's hiding place.

> Blessed is the one whose transgression is forgiven, whose sin is covered. Blessed is the man against whom the Lord counts no iniquity, and in whose spirit there is no deceit. For when I kept silent, my bones wasted away through my groaning all day long. (Psalm 32:1- 3)

How does God's forgiveness feel? In Psalm 32:7 David writes: "You are a hiding place for me; You preserve me from trouble; You surround me with shouts of deliverance." David says that after his confession and God's forgiveness, he is hidden in God, feeling safe and surrounded with shouts of deliverance. Could there be any sound better than shouts of deliverance to a person who has felt so burdened by their misdeeds?

Psalm 32:10 reveals the key to confession and forgiveness: "Steadfast love surrounds the one who trusts in the Lord." Trust in a loving Father is key. If we don't trust, then we won't feel the security to own up to our mess. No one wants to stay in hiding. *As David testifies, concealing sin produces stress, guilt, shame, and fear. In humility, David uncovered and acknowledged all of his wrongs. If being surrounded by steadfast love and shouts of deliverance sound good to you, understand you will not experience this without trust, humility, and confession.*

SERVING THE PURPOSE OF GOD

After David admits his wrongdoing, he feels the freedom of forgiveness and he can share the collateral blessing of his errors, the teaching he offers that brings glory to God. Here in Psalm 32, David wants to guide others to confess, to come out of hiding.

Acts 13:36 says that David "served the purpose of God in his generation." Wouldn't you want that to be said about you? *Your messy life can and should become your message.* You can bless others with the story of your redemption and the renewal of your life, with stories of the shouts of deliverance you have heard.

God has allowed each of us to follow a different road to get to where we walk today. He has allowed both good and bad along our path, and everything can be used by God for His purposes. Don't waste the brokenness becoming beauty in your story. Many people think their sin disqualifies them from serving a purpose in God's kingdom. If we learn anything from David's life, we can see the capability of God to work through any life. Let's return to my question about an adulterous murderer being called "a man after God's own heart." Yes, David committed horrible wrongs, but he confessed and shouldered his wrongdoing without shifting blame. David bore his shame, but most importantly, he didn't want to waste the teaching opportunity of his unrighteous choices. He still wanted purpose in the kingdom of God.

God crafted your life. Just like King David, He can use all of your mess for good. But you have to trust Him to do that. Are you hearing those distant shouts of deliverance? Are they getting louder?

JOY AND FREEDOM IN THE LORD

David lived a life marked by extreme highs and lows, but ultimately God used David's story to illustrate the joy and freedom found in forgiveness. Throughout the Psalms, we hear David proclaim that joy:

> Psalm 5:11—But let all who take refuge in you rejoice; let them ever sing for joy, and spread your protection over them, that those who love your name may exult in you.

> Psalm 32:11—Be glad in the Lord, and rejoice, O righteous, and shout for joy, all you upright in heart!

We are healed from the deep pain of our sin by seeking and experiencing God's forgiveness. Dr. John MacArthur writes: "Forgiveness is a healthy, wholesome, virtuous, liberating act. Forgiveness unleashes joy. It brings peace. It washes the slate clean."[24]

When David's confession freed him from his hiding place, and he could feel God's forgiveness, he could finally rejoice in the Lord.

David also encouraged others to leave their secret places to join him in freedom and worship of God.

THE ONE WHO SETS THE PRISONERS FREE

In the book of Luke, we learn that right after Jesus spent 40 days in the wilderness being tempted by Satan, He visits the synagogue in His hometown of Nazareth. That Sabbath day, Jesus reads Isaiah 61:1-2, and He says these verses summarize His mission on Earth. Here's how Luke recorded what Jesus said: "The Spirit of the Lord is on me, because He has anointed me to proclaim good news to the poor. He has sent me to proclaim freedom for the prisoners

JESUS'S MARCHING ORDERS WERE TO PROCLAIM GOOD NEWS, PROCLAIM FREEDOM, TO GIVE SIGHT TO THE BLIND, AND TO FREE THOSE WHO ARE OPPRESSED.

and recovery of sight for the blind, to set the oppressed free" (Luke 4:18 NIV).

Jesus's marching orders were to proclaim good news, proclaim freedom, to give sight to the blind, and to free those who are oppressed. All of these assignments given to Him have to do with freeing humans from the wrongs they have done. Jesus didn't come to Earth to make life temporarily easier for people. Jesus came to free prisoners from their sin permanently, and to bring them everlasting joy.

That joy comes to us when we trust Jesus with our lives, and we ask for forgiveness. When we allow Jesus's Holy Spirit to shine His Light into our hiding place, we can be assured of forgiveness, and we can, like David, live in freedom and joy, hearing shouts of deliverance.

When each of us knows freedom from sin and freedom from hiding, we have great reason to celebrate the One who sets us free. We leave behind guilt and shame in the destruction of our hiding place.

For Discussion

1. David's prayer in Psalm 139:23-24 is a bold prayer because it opens a person up to an intimate revelation of their sin life. The prayer humbly asks God to search one's heart, but the prayer also states a willingness to be led in God's path. Share your feelings about praying this for yourself.

_____

_____

_____

_____

_____

2. David knows there is nowhere to hide from God, and he writes of this in Psalm 139:7. Yet, David made attempts to hide his grievous sins. Obviously, he forgot (or ignored) what he knew to be true. Share about a time you went down a path of forgetting or ignoring God as David did.

_____

_____

_____

_____

_____

3. God allows purpose in our pain. In Psalm 51:12-13, David pleads with God to give him the opportunity to "teach transgressors Your ways." Where do you see purpose in the pain of your wrongdoing?

_____

_____

_____

_____

_____

_____

4. Psalm 32 begins with David reflecting on the blessing of forgiveness, on the blessing of sin being covered (remember Adam, Eve and the prodigal son being covered?). In Psalm 32:7, David writes God surrounds with "shouts of deliverance." Share when you have heard those shouts.

_____

_____

_____

_____

_____

5. Another of David's psalms mentions joy being found in God's refuge. (Psalm 5:11) Jesus said His marching orders were to bring good news to the poor and oppressed, and to set captives free. Our hiding places are exactly what Christ came to break down. Share anything that holds you back from partnering with Christ's Holy Spirit in breaking down the walls of your hiding place.

_____

_____

_____

_____

_____

_____

CHAPTER 9

CONFESSIONAL

STORYTELLING

Confess your sins to each other and pray for each other so God can heal you. When a believing person prays, great things happen.

James 5:16 NCV

Christ Jesus came into the world to save sinners, of whom I am the foremost.

Paul, the Apostle - 1 Timothy 1:15

THE COUPLE STANDING in front of the church were married, but on this Sunday, you wouldn't know that by the distance between them. The tension in Steve and Jenn's marriage was painfully evident as Steve began to tell his story. Through his tears, he shared a gut-wrenching story of his path into sexual addiction and extramarital affairs.

Steve grew up being raised by his two older brothers without close attention from parents who worked constantly. By the sixth-grade, Steve drank and shared Playboy pictures with his friends.

Like me, Steve headed off to a small Christian college with a broken moral compass. While there, Steve met Mary, the woman who would become his first wife. When they moved to Southern California, Steve and Mary connected to a young, growing church, and became leaders of a small group. But the marriage had issues, and Steve's eye started to wander.

Steve worked as a sales rep in an industry that often had regional and national sales meetings. At one of these gatherings he became involved in an extramarital affair. Significant guilt and shame followed Steve's indiscretions, and he felt compelled to confess the affair to Mary. When Steve confessed, Mary revealed some things she had been concealing as well, though nothing she was hiding led her to a sexual affair.

The marriage wasn't ready for a child, but Mary became pregnant, and when the child arrived, the responsibilities of motherhood overwhelmed her. She joined a gym and pursued social activities which took her further away from Steve and their child. The marriage didn't last, and Steve was single again.

A friend at work turned Steve on to online pornography, and he was hooked. Match.com provided Steve with an endless supply of casual sexual relationships. Steve could pass for a professional male model, and that didn't help. Ironically, he pursed this lifestyle while going to the same church he had attended with Mary.

At a local bar, Steve met Jenn, and they fell hard for each other. Their relationship turned more complex when Jenn became pregnant. They became engaged, but behind the scenes, Steve still visited local massage parlors and continued having affairs at corporate sales meetings.

While going through premarital counseling, Steve's internal moral conflict became greater than he could bear, and he confessed some, but not all, of his sexual activities to his pastor. The pastor encouraged Steve to set a date by which he would offer a full confession to Jenn. Steve eventually confessed to her about his porn addiction and the massage parlor visits but held back sharing anything about his relationships with other women.

After joining a 12-step program for sex addicts, and with further encouragement from his pastor, Steve came to realize he needed to share everything with Jenn (who was now five months pregnant with their second child). When he offered a full disclosure, Steve felt as if a great weight had been lifted off his shoulders, but the revelation crushed Jenn. She demanded Steve go to rehab to get help, and then Jenn shocked Steve by leaving California temporarily to live with her parents out of state.

Jenn returned to California to have a home birth for their child and allowed Steve to join in on the delivery of their son. Over the next few weeks, Jenn saw a different character in Steve than she had seen before. Steve was becoming a more humble and transparent man. The Holy Spirit led Jenn to forgive Steve for everything he had confessed, and they began working with counselors to unravel the damage which had been done in their marriage.

That Sunday, both Steve and Jenn ended their stories with an offering of gratitude that the Holy Spirit had blessed them with a renewed relationship. As they finished speaking, the room was hushed, but applause quickly broke through the stillness. The congregation wasn't applauding Steve's wrongdoing, they applauded his courage in his transparency. As Steve and Jenn walked back to their seats, I don't think there was a dry eye in the room.

We felt as if had known this couple's pain, and we wanted to come alongside to support them. You could sense the tension between the two, but you could also see healing on the move. What a powerful testimony to the work of the Holy Spirit in the lives of people striving to follow Christ, willing to be so transparent.

CONFESSIONAL STORYTELLING

How rare is it to hear a public confession like Steve's in a church setting? But how beautiful. For Steve to stand before our congregation and own up to his hiding place required courage through much discomfort, but his transparency encouraged many others to be equally vulnerable. That's just a glimpse of confessional storytelling, and what it might look like in the context of "church."

HOW RARE IS IT TO HEAR A PUBLIC CONFESSION LIKE STEVE'S IN A CHURCH SETTING? BUT HOW BEAUTIFUL.

Every believer has a story to tell. We each have a story about struggling with our sinful flesh and its desires, and the challenge we face to push back against that force in our life. These revealing stories also can show how God has patiently loved us through our lusts and our disobedience.

Confessional storytelling isn't "normal" in a church setting, but it should be. If churches pursued confession as a common practice and became as transparent and "real" as an AA meeting or a Celebrate Recovery gathering, imagine what changes could occur in our church family. In *Why We Eat Our Own*, Michael Cheshire says: "Normally, someone will argue this is not the appropriate setting to discuss a private matter between two people. Oh, come on! We are not going to change church culture by being appropriate. In fact, we need to be less appropriate and more authentic."[25]

Normalizing an admission of wrongs is the first step in our individual and corporate healing. If we humbly embraced the truth that we are all sinners in need of a Savior, and we are willing to push away our pride, we might just have a fighting chance to make confession the norm, and not the exception.

A Confessional Community?

One of Dietrich Bonhoeffer's favorite subjects was how we can minister to each other through hearing one another's confession and assuring each other of our forgiveness before God:

"As long as I am by myself when I confess my sins, everything remains in the dark; but when I come face to face with another Christian, the sin has to be brought to light...As the acknowledgment of my sins to another believer frees me from the grip of self-deception, so too, the promise of forgiveness becomes fully certain to me when it is spoken by another believer as God's command and in God's name. Confession before one another is given to us by God so that we might be assured of divine forgiveness"[26]

Make note of Bonhoeffer's statement about confession freeing us from the grip of self-deception. Look back at the cover of this book you are holding. The subtitle is: "God's Plan to Free You from Guilt and Shame." God's plan for our freedom includes confessing to one another, as well as the assurance of forgiveness and accountability we can offer each other. God gave us this gift, and we need to open the gift often. But this change requires us to adopt a different DNA. We need a new DNA that embraces confession.

When all of us work to cover up our sin, we undermine growing deeper in community. The greater the extent of hiding, the shallower our relationships will be. In not sharing our struggles, we put up a false front—a facade—and our lack of transparency encourages others to do the same. We build walls. We become prideful silos, interested only in appearances. We also become lonely silos. We don't share our deeper needs, and we also don't hear of other's burdens in the community of faith. When we aren't aware of other's needs, it's impossible to come alongside them. The flip side of this equation is true as well. If we have made no effort to share our struggle, when we are most in need, there is no brother or sister to come alongside us.

DNA CHANGE BEGINS WITH YOU

When asked a question about the greatest commandment, here's what Jesus said: "'You must love the Lord your God with all your heart, all your soul, and all your mind.' This is the first and greatest commandment. A second is equally important: 'Love your neighbor as yourself'" (Matthew 22:37 NLT). The Apostle Paul expanded on our calling as Christians: "Let us think of ways to motivate one another to acts of love and good works" (Hebrews 10:24 NLT).

We have a calling to be salt and light in the world, and if we are cowering in silos, we fail in that calling. We want to love one another, bear each other's burdens, and motivate each other to love and good works. When we pursue these things, we bring glory to our God, which is how we show our love for Him to the world.

We need help to get back on the right path when we mess up.

REVEALING PERSONAL WRONGS TO OTHERS HAS TO START WITH THE OPPOSITE OF PRIDE.

Paul reminds us: "Dear brothers and sisters, if another believer is overcome by some sin, you who are godly should gently and humbly help that person back onto the right path." (Gal. 6:1a NLT) We need to humbly ask for the help of our brothers and sisters, and we need to seek ways we can cooperate with the Holy Spirit in strengthening our resolve to walk closely with our Savior.

Many of us see the value of hearing another believer's revelation of their brokenness, and we see the beauty of extending the love and forgiveness of Christ to that brother or sister. But here's the problem:

While we see the need for transparency, we lack the motivation to take the risk to pursue it ourselves. What a wonderful and necessary ministry this might be. Hearing another's confession and assuring them of God's forgiveness is so valuable in our lives.

Revealing personal wrongs to others has to start with the opposite of pride. But Satan hates humility. He doesn't like it when you own up to your ugly stuff, because when you put your sin out there in the open, out on the table for others to help, something great could happen:

You might deal with it.

THE 'METHOD' OF JOHN WESLEY

In the eighteenth century, John Wesley served as a pastor and theologian in England. Wesley believed confession, repentance, and mutual accountability are fundamental to the church's growth and strength. In his opinion, this was the key to holiness in the body of Christ. Wesley knew the only way to accomplish the intimacy he felt would facilitate the admission of wrongs was through the formation of small groups he called "the bands." These groups became the cornerstone of the early Methodist Church.

The bands came together as groups of either men or women and usually had six to seven members. In these gatherings, confession could occur without the fear of condemnation. They would meet together weekly, and would hold each other accountable with these five questions:

1. What known sins have you committed since our last meeting?

2. What temptations have you faced this week?

3. How were you delivered from giving into these temptations?

4. What have you thought, said or done that made you wonder if it was a sin?

5. Is there anything you are hiding as a secret sin?

Can you imagine how the DNA of our churches would change if each of us willingly held each other accountable this way on a weekly basis? The people of the bands believed in and followed the commandment in the book of James: "Confess your sins to each other and pray for each other so God can heal you. When a believing person prays, great things happen" (James 5:16-NCV). They heard each other's confession, held each other accountable, and prayed for each other. The structure of the bands stayed in place within the Methodist Church for over 100 years, and out of these gatherings grew an entire Christian denomination.

THE CHURCH REPURPOSED

When we look back at the first-century Church in the book of Acts, we can't help but be struck by the contrast with the Church of today. We have been drained of our power, and we have willingly allowed this to happen. We need to ask ourselves why this might be. Three reasons present themselves.

The first is our pride is holding us back from coming out of our hiding places.

The second reason is because we don't put our transformed lives on display for a broken world to see.

The third reason is we haven't been intentional as John Wesley was in creating a safe space to share our hidden life. Nothing will change until that happens.

We need the help of the community of faith so we can spur each other on to godliness. Ed Welch writes: "Spiritual battles cannot be fought alone. Even though it seems much easier to keep our struggles private or to reveal them only to those with similar ones, we need the diverse ministries of the church of Jesus Christ. This is God's intent."[27]

What if followers of Christ lived disarmingly transparent lives in the face of an unbelieving world? What kind of a difference might we see?

The body of Christ here on Earth (the Church) needs to be way less concerned about our Sunday best "Facebook image," and more concerned about being

WE NEED THE HELP OF THE COMMUNITY OF FAITH SO WE CAN SPUR EACH OTHER ON TO GODLINESS.

transparent sinners focused on loving God and loving others.

HOW DOES GOD USE A SINNER LIKE ME FOR GOOD WORKS?

A number of Bible verses tell us we each have a purpose in God's Kingdom, in spite of all of the wrong things we might have done:

> For we are God's masterpiece. He has created us anew in Christ Jesus, so we can do the good things He planned for us long ago (Ephesians 2:10 NLT).
>
> If you keep yourself pure, you will be a special utensil for honorable use. Your life will be clean, and you will be ready for the Master to use you for every good work (2 Timothy 2:21 NLT).

God's Word is true. God can use you if you have lived a life full of wrongdoing. You might not feel God made you as His masterpiece, or as His special utensil, but the discouraging voice whispering that message in your ear does not come from God, the message comes from Satan, our enemy.

When you pursue unrighteous living, God still has a plan for you. You just don't realize it yet. God is eager to use your life, which He crafted specifically for His plan. He has a path just for you to bring Him honor.

Let Your Mess Be Your Message

God allowed you to experience everything you have gone through

All of your life can be used in your message, in your testimony.

in your life. He allowed you to live through painful experiences so your dependence on Him would grow deeper and you could grow in endurance. In his book *Trusting God*, author Jerry Bridges shares this point: "God's plan for us is not contingent on our decisions. God's plan is not contingent at all. God's plan is sovereign. It includes our foolish decisions as well as our wise ones."[28]

All of your life can be used in your message, in your testimony. You will make God smile when you see His hand in your life, and when you tell others about how He loved you through the pain you have experienced.

Messy Stories God Used

If you remain unconvinced God can use you and the collateral blessing of your mess for His purposes, I want to remind you of a few of the people in the Bible God used for His glory, though they had made a mess of their lives:

Peter, the Apostle—I love Peter, a hot-headed follower of Christ who shoots his mouth off, lives to regret it, but rallies in the end. Peter got fired up for Christ, enough to walk with Him on water! But standing around a fire in the courtyard of the high priest the night of Jesus's arrest, he melts into a coward (temporarily). He denies being associated with Jesus, not once, but three times. Then the cock crows, and Peter realizes just how far away from Christ he has allowed his fear to take him. His response is understandable: he "wept bitterly."

John 21 tells us when Christ rose from the dead, He met up with Peter beside another fire on the shore of Lake Tiberias and took the opportunity to reassure Peter. Three times, Christ asks Peter if he loves Him. Christ wants Peter to know he's forgiven.

We read in Acts 2 that within just weeks of those fireside denials and reassurances, Peter boldly preaches a sermon on Pentecost in the middle of Jerusalem. This isn't friendly territory, but Peter goes for it. Where did the cowardly apostle go? He's a new man. Because of his Spirit-filled preaching that day, more than 3,000 people become followers of Christ, and the Church is born. *Collateral blessing.*

Moses—At 40, Moses murders an Egyptian he found beating an Israelite slave. Exodus 3 tells us Moses fled in fear to the desert where he lived for 40 years as a shepherd before God appeared to him in the burning bush and gives him his marching orders.

GOD CHOSE A MURDERING SHEPHERD WITH LITTLE CONFIDENCE TO LEAD HIS CHOSEN PEOPLE OUT OF EGYPT, AND TO THE PROMISED LAND.

I love God's sense of humor: Moses was 80 when God tapped him on the shoulder with a crazy plan...lead another flock of sheep for 40 more years (this time it would be over a million Israelites). God chose a murdering shepherd with little confidence to lead His chosen people out of Egypt, and to the Promised Land. *Collateral blessing.*

King David—As a young man, David lived as a man after God's own heart, but he became a self-absorbed adulterer and murderer. After he committed adultery and murder, he wrote a significant number of Psalms that bless us with a great deal of wisdom and understanding. He fathered Solomon, the wisest man who lived during the Old Testament times, and Solomon passed on his father's wisdom and his own in the book of Proverbs. *Collateral blessing.*

The Woman at the Well—When I get to heaven, I'm going to look up this woman, just to find out what her name is. Jesus met a woman by "Jacob's well" while passing through Samaria, and engages her in conversation. The woman realizes Jesus has the ability to prophesy, because He reveals a whole lot about her story…way more than any stranger would know. This woman has lived a rather sketchy life, having had five husbands, and she's living with a man that's not her husband. After a little time conversing with Jesus, she is convinced He is the Messiah predicted for centuries, and she runs back to her village to call everyone to meet this prophetic stranger. The townspeople convince Jesus to stay in their village for a few days, and John 4:41 tells us many more in the town heard Jesus's message, and came to faith…all because of this unnamed woman. *Collateral blessing.*

Now most of you reading this book have not killed anyone, and I doubt many of you have been married five times, but the Bible testifies God can use people who have done some messy things. Isaiah writes on behalf of God: "Bring all who claim me as their God, for I have made them for my glory. It was I who created them" (Isaiah 43:7 NLT).

CATCH-22

Remember the story I told of Katherine and Eric? Their lives were changed because of the humble, transparent story told by a pastor who has since gone on to be with the Lord. That man's courage in sharing his past struggles brought at least two people to a saving faith, and likely, many more were also affected.

A survey done in 2011 by the online magazine *Church Leaders* revealed 68% of the 500 pastors surveyed did not have anyone they felt they could confess to, and 66% expressed a fear that discussing

172 | MARK BRANDES

their struggles with sin from the pulpit would put their ministry at risk. In the same article, writer and pastor Ron Forseth made this observation:

> In light of the 68% of church leaders that indicated they rarely or never confess their sins to another, we get a glimpse of the unique dilemma pastors face. Even as they *must* confess their sins, pastors don't feel they *can* confess their sins because of the risks it brings to their ministries. So the perceived catch is this: we can't win.[29]

Our DNA can't change until pastors are able to stand before their congregations to share their struggles. But wait: Why would they do that if the rest of us sitting out in the pews and the chairs don't make it safe for them to share? Is this the Catch-22 for confession in our twenty-first-century church?

CONFESSIONAL LEADERS

Those of us sitting in the chairs or pews on Sunday mornings aren't the only ones who need to pursue confessional storytelling. The person teaching up front also needs to have a safe place to confess.

Pastors have struggles, too. Just ask Max Lucado. You probably know Max from one of his 42 (and counting) books you see when you're browsing through the Christian section at Barnes and Noble Booksellers. Lucado serves at Oak Hills Church in San Antonio, Texas, and is a well-known author. In 2012, Pastor Lucado wrote an article for *Christianity Today,* about a struggle he had with drinking. He had grown up loving to drink beer, but as his responsibilities in the church grew, he had decided he could no longer partake as he had in the past. For years, Pastor Lucado didn't drink at all, but he slipped into a short period of habitual drinking, to the point of sitting in his car in the parking lot of a convenience store with an open beer hidden in a brown paper bag. In the *Christianity Today* article, Max shared how he became convicted of his sin, and how he came forward to confess, not only to his elder board, but also to his entire congregation. Here's a quote from Lucado's article which speaks specifically to pastors:

> Instill in your congregation the importance of confession. Avoid fostering the image that your fellowship is full of perfect people (you won't fit in). Instead, show by example a church where members and leaders alike confess their sins and show humility, where the price of admission is simply an admission of guilt. Healing happens in a church like this. Grace happens in a church like this. Followers of Christ have been given authority to hear confession and proclaim grace. Confessors find a freedom that deniers don't. And confessing pastors lead freedom-filled churches.[30]

The price of admission is simply an admission of guilt. I love that thought. Thank God Max Lucado willingly stood before his congregation, shared his burden of sin, but also blessed many more with writing about it in a national magazine for other pastors. He could have kept the issue private within his church body, but he offered up the collateral blessing of his testimony for the benefit of others.

CONFESSORS CHANGE DNA

From Lucado's quote above, we might assume he agrees with Bonhoeffer's perspective on confession among believers: "Followers of Christ have been given authority to hear confession and proclaim grace." Listen to the echo of Bonhoeffer as Lucado points to the freedom found in transparent admissions of guilt: *"Confessors find a freedom that deniers don't. And confessing pastors lead freedom-filled churches."*

Pastors and church leaders need to model a humble admission of their failings. We will only see a DNA change when our pastors model transparency and encourage the church to do the same. *If we want to be intentional about this change, our churches must become places of safety and refuge—for pastors as well as parishioners.* What if this became a way of life for the Christian faith? What if we put aside our pride, and lived out confessional storytelling? I'm not saying it always has to be in front of the church, but what an inspiration it is when that happens.

WE WILL ONLY SEE A DNA CHANGE WHEN OUR PASTORS MODEL TRANSPARENCY AND ENCOURAGE THE CHURCH TO DO THE SAME.

If you follow Christ and agree the DNA of the church needs to change, then, first and foremost, you need to be a part of a movement to make it safe for your pastor and leaders to draw us all into confessional storytelling. This might require you to take those leaders off any pedestal you might have placed them on, and to remind yourself church leaders are sinners just like you and me. If you see weaknesses in their lives, show them the same grace, mercy, and forgiveness you desire.

WE HAVE WORK TO DO

Within the Christian faith, we need to examine how to address our sin, as well as our pastor's sin. As a biblical counselor, I would propose every church have a counseling ministry using God's Word as its foundation. Only the Word of God drills down to our heart's deepest needs.

Everyone has a role to play in changing the Body of Christ to become a safe place for real admission of guilt. This won't happen if we just sit around hoping others will take the initiative to be the first to share their story. We need to commit to this, not for a week, not for a series of sermons, but for decades to come. *Only when we make confessional storytelling a norm will our churches be the refuge God intended them to be.*

For Discussion

1. Jesus gave us our own marching orders, which are to love God and our neighbor. (Matthew 22:37) In the Christian faith, "loving our neighbor" includes confessing our sins and praying for one another. (James 5:16) Share why you believe we have a difficult time following these commands.

_____

_____

_____

_____

_____

_____

2. Imagine that churches followed James 5:16. How do you think your church would change?

_____

_____

_____

_____

_____

_____

3. There is a risk in confession, but there is a blessing as well. Share how you might be blessed to be a confessor. How might you be blessed, or bless another in hearing someone else's confession?

_____

_____

_____

_____

_____

_____

4. Followers of Christ are told to restore anyone caught in a transgression in a spirit of gentleness. (Galatians 6:1) Why are we often reluctant to restore? Why might we feel as if we need to hand out discipline to others?

_____

_____

_____

_____

_____

_____

5. Hebrews 10:24 offers additional marching orders. Believers are to "stir one another to love and good works." Share how you would feel about others stirring you to love and good works. Are you willing to stir others? What would this require on the part of both parties?

_____

_____

_____

_____

_____

_____

CHAPTER 10

REPURPOSED

If I had cherished sin in my heart, the Lord would not have listened.

Psalm 66:18 NIV

Give me one hundred preachers who fear nothing but sin and desire nothing but God, and I care not whether they be clergymen or laymen, they alone will shake the gates of Hell and set up the kingdom of Heaven upon Earth.

John Wesley

I TURNED 16 March 10, 1969, and got my driver's license the same day. My father owned a 1963 VW Bug, and a 1967 Buick Wildcat (though they called it a "Wildcat," it had four doors and drove like a boat). Neither of these cars prepared me for the ride I took in the summer of '69.

Back in Texas, I had a cousin named Cathy whose father had just given her a brand new 1969 Plymouth GTX with a 440 Magnum engine. For those of you who have no idea what kind of beast this is, let me fill you in. The dealerships sold the GTX as a "gentleman's muscle car," and its engine developed 375 horsepower, capable of doing 0-60 in 6.5 seconds. I guess that would be helpful if Cathy ran late getting into town for cheerleading practice.

There's something else you need to know about the GTX. It sounded mean. *Dangerously* mean. With a big, fire breathing engine under the hood, the exhaust sounded incredibly raw, and that free flow allowed the car to run like a bat out of Hades. Remember, this was back in the day when "noise pollution" wasn't a big deal.

Trinity Lutheran Church sits on Texas Highway 2301 about 12 miles outside of Lockney, Texas. If you looked it up on Google Maps, a wonderful mosaic of farming properties surrounds the church. I know my relatives would be insulted if they heard me say it's in the middle of nowhere, but it is.

On a hot Sunday in July of 1969, I stood outside Trinity Lutheran with my cousins, Alfred and Charlie, admiring Cathy's new ride. Perhaps it was the drool forming on the corner of my lip that tipped Cathy off we would be interested in having her take us for a spin.

Cathy told us to hop in, and before we knew it, we were headed toward Plainview, Texas going 100 mph. I'd never been in a car going that fast. Cathy must have caught a glimpse of more drool, because she turned to me and asked if I'd like to have a go behind the wheel of the GTX. Would I? What kind of a question is that? Of course!

West Texas farm roads run as straight as an arrow, so Cathy figured there wasn't much of a chance I'd end up in a ditch or tear through some farmer's pasture fence. I started out driving a bit cautiously, but with some encouragement from all my cousins in the car, I wound that baby up to just a bit over 110 mph until I came over a slight hill and realized there were train tracks ahead.

That day, no train challenged us to slow from 110 mph to a dead stop in 4 seconds (thank God), but you have to know this…all train tracks have a slight elevation. When you're doing the 60 mph speed limit, that 2-foot incline doesn't make much of a difference.

However…when you're going 100+ mph, that small rise becomes a launchpad.

I'm sure I got all four wheels off the ground for *at least five seconds*. Okay, maybe just for a half-second. I might have embellished the story over these 50 years, but I can tell you I've not had a more thrilling ride. We all made it back to the church in one piece, hearts still  racing, but that car scared the snot out of me. Fun but scary.

Cars today have so many devices that rob an engine of its true raw power, not like back in 1969. Those devices help our air quality and give us better gas mileage (the GTX got under 10 mpg when playing around). Some cars come with a governor to keep from hitting railroad tracks at 110 mph, but they're power robbers.

POWER ROBBERS IN CHRIST'S CHURCH

Many people rob the church of power today, and I am guilty of this, too. When we hide our wrongdoing, we rob the church of the power of Jesus. God can't use us as He would like when habitual sin has its grip on us. We don't hear or respond to the Holy Spirit because our brokenness causes us to go spiritually deaf.

GOD CAN'T USE US AS HE WOULD LIKE WHEN HABITUAL SIN HAS ITS GRIP ON US.

Psalm 66 tells us: "If I had cherished sin in my heart, the Lord would not have listened; but God has surely listened and has heard my prayer. Praise be to God, who has not rejected my prayer or withheld his love from me!" (Psalm 66:18-20 NIV). How appropriate the psalmist used the phrase "cherished sin." In an earlier chapter, I talked about how our love of darkness causes us to coddle sin. That's just what cherishing wrongdoing looks like. When we hold on to our unconfessed brokenness, we cherish or coddle our fleshly desires. Coddling and hiding sin rob Christ's church of power.

A COMMUNITY OF FORGIVEN SINNERS

If our community of Christ followers expects to "regain our roar," that can only begin when we come out of hiding, out of our silos, and face each other in humility. When that happens, our flesh and our sin lose the ability to trip us up, and the true power of Christ's love and forgiveness illuminates our community. Dietrich Bonhoeffer says it well:

> Sin that has been spoken and confessed has lost all of its pow-
> er...It can no longer tear apart the community...The sinner
> has been relieved of sin's burden...We can admit our sins and
> in this very act find community for the first time. The hidden
> sins separated the sinner from the community and made the
> sinner's apparent community all a sham. The sins that were
> acknowledged helped the sinner to find true community with
> other believers in Jesus Christ.[31]

When this happens, when hiding places and silos are broken down, the world will be stunned because the followers of Christ will stand in sharp contrast to all that surrounds them. When this happens, some will be repulsed, but many in the world will react as Katherine and Eric did and say, "If this is what Christianity looks like here, we want in."

GOD'S GLORY

We should be convicted by this quote from pastor and author John Piper: "What you love determines what you feel shame about. If you love for men to make much of you, you will feel shame when they don't. But if you love for men to make much of Christ, then you will feel shame if He is belittled on your account."[32] Do I live that way? Am I that concerned about the progress of my personal transformation and how it may or may not reflect well on Christ?

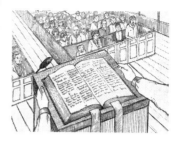

When followers of Christ hide their wrongs, they might not consider what the world "outside" Christianity thinks. But we should.

C.S. Lewis wrote: "When we Christians behave badly, or fail to behave well, we are making Christianity unbelievable to the outside world...Our careless lives set the outer world talking; and we give them grounds for talking in a way that throws doubt on the truth of Christianity itself."[33] What a sad statement, but we know it's true. I don't want anything in my life to cast doubt on the truth of the Christian faith, and I would hope you would feel the same.

God gets the glory when sinners confess, when they repent, and when their lives become more like Christ's. This is a miracle, and the working of the Holy Spirit in their lives is the cause. We shouldn't get the glory for our transformation, God should. When this happens, what can the world say in response?

Think of what a difference a culture of confession would make in how those outside our faith view followers of Christ. Can you imagine the experience of visitors to our gatherings as they stand in amazement at our transparency, our love for each other, and our love for them? Instead of being thought of as a bunch of "holier than thou" people who look down their noses at others who don't have it as "together," our churches could be seen as safe places filled with people who do what the Bible says: *We bear each other's burdens, we strive to live like Christ, and we give God the glory for the transformation.*

Rejoice with Me

In the prodigal son story, the father didn't have to kill the fatted calf to feed the entire village. He didn't have to be so extravagant. The father could have just hugged the prodigal and put him to work alongside his older brother in the field, but he didn't. Jesus wanted to make a point. *God's amazing love for us makes hiding unnecessary. His forgiveness welcomes us back into the family of God.*

The three parables Jesus told in Luke 15 vary in the details of what/who was lost, but they all have common themes. In all three stories, the community comes together to rejoice over the return of the lost sheep, the lost coin, and the lost son.

When we hide sin, we become lost in the dark places of our life.

In every story, something or someone is lost. When we hide sin, we become lost in the dark places of our life. *The light of Christ in our lives becomes dim, and we aren't able to hear the Holy Spirit's prompting us toward good works.*

Why did Jesus make all three celebrations in Luke 15 public events? In these parables, Christ encourages us to celebrate repentant, confessional stories as a testimony for both followers of Christ as well as those outside of the faith. *When we share confessional stories that praise and honor God for His forgiving heart, we encourage others to step into God's good plans made specifically for them.*

Sin should not be celebrated, but we should rejoice when people find freedom from their need to hide because of the One who covers their guilt and the shame of their wrongs. Through His intentional, loving grace and forgiveness, secured by the blood He shed on a cross outside of Jerusalem, Jesus covers over our sin and sets us free.

Confession begins this journey out of hiding, and we need to create safe spaces for shouldering our wrongs.

TWENTY-FIRST-CENTURY BANDS

We need revival in the twenty-first-century Church. Revival brings our attention back to the good news of Christ's sacrifice, His forgiveness, and the freedom we find there. The Holy Spirit works in revival by convicting Christ followers to live godly lives, and confession plays a significant role in conviction. Today, we need a safe place for confession that includes accountability and encouragement. Both women and men of Christ need to become "iron sharpening iron."

What if the Christian Church of the twenty-first century reestablished the "bands"? Would we see followers of Christ drawn into a closer relationship with Him and with each other? Could intimate confessional groups cause revival to break out? What if groups of women and men gathered weekly, and posed these questions:

1. What prayers can we offer on each other's behalf?

2. What's the question you don't want us to ask you?

3. Can we offer you assurance of God's forgiveness when you confess?

4. What good work is God calling you to pursue?

5. How can we help move you along the path God has placed before you?

These questions focus on 1) our need for prayer in the present, 2) our admission of past sins and the assurance of our forgiveness, and 3) our purpose for our Lord in the future.

These weekly gatherings have the potential of freeing us from habitual sins holding us back from fully engaging in the good works

God has planned for us. *If we held each other accountable and motivated each other toward godliness, imagine what a difference we might make in the world. Could this be the DNA change we desperately need?*

People Repurposed

Often, at a baptism of adults, the pastor might encourage the people being baptized to share a bit about themselves and their decision to follow Christ. Here's what will bring me to tears: put a microphone in the hand of a 70-year-old-man who just came to Christ and let him tell his story. For me, there's nothing better than to hear the story of a conversion to Jesus happening later in life.

A PERSON WHO HAS LIVED A LONG LIFE SEPARATED FROM GOD, AND WHO HAS ACCEPTED JESUS AS SAVIOR HAS A POWERFUL, DEEP STORY TO TELL.

A person who has lived a long life separated from God, and who has accepted Jesus as Savior has a powerful, deep story to tell. These people give context to the redemptive value of Christ's death and resurrection. Gratitude for God's love is huge for these people, and often they express this wistful thought: "I wish I had known Jesus all my life!"

Here's the beauty of a testimony like this: At a later date in their lives, these people have found their true purpose. Previously, they occupied their heart's throne instead of allowing Jesus Christ His rightful place. When you put Jesus on the throne of your life, everything makes sense, and you find your purpose.

YOUR FINEST HOUR

Dennis Rainey is an author and the cofounder of FamilyLife, a ministry of Campus Crusade for Christ (Cru). He wrote a small but impactful book titled *Choosing a Life That Matters*. I highly recommend it to everyone, especially the final chapter, "Serve God, Not Self." I love this quote: "There comes into the life of every person a task for which he or she is uniquely suited. What a shame if that moment finds us either unwilling or unprepared for that which could become what Churchill referred to as "our finest hour."[34]

THE LIFE YOU HAVE
EXPERIENCED HAS
LEFT YOU "UNIQUELY
SUITED" FOR THE
GOOD WORKS GOD
HAS PREPARED
ONLY FOR YOU.

The life you have experienced has left you "uniquely suited" for the good works God has prepared only for you. If you are young when you come to realize this truth, you are blessed to have the potential of many years left to give glory to God with your life.

Rick Warren writes: "As you grow closer to Him [God], He will give you a passion for something He cares about deeply so you can be a spokesman for Him in the world. It may be a passion about a problem, a purpose, a principle, or a group of people. Whatever it is, you will feel compelled to speak up about it and do what you can to make a difference."[35]

The passion of which Rick Warren wrote in his book *The Purpose Driven Life* only occurs when people come out of hiding. When that happens, people are free to be led by the Spirit of God to explore their life purposes, the good works God created them to do.

This is the ultimate goal of re-creating "the bands." Good works that honor God reflect Christ in our world, and we are called to this.

When you pursue freedom and your "passion with purpose" rises, you begin to live for God's glory, not your own. Repurposed for your finest hour with God.

Followers of Christ live as forgiven sinners whose ultimate purpose is to honor God with their lives. Everyone needs help along the way of this pursuit. We need to lead each other in confession as well as spurring each other toward love and good works.

Pastors should see themselves as God's messenger of His Word, but they also play an important role in focusing the passions and purposes of their flock. Sheep need a leader to follow, and they need a model for confession.

PASTORS:

- Your church body needs you to be courageous in how you model confession. Your flock needs you to humbly point to some of your struggles and share how you have worked to deal with them in your life. *Share it.*

- Teach the Word of God, and demonstrate that throughout Scripture, God has revealed His desire for confession and healing. We are all like sheep, and we forget. As a shepherd of a flock, your job is to remind us to transparently share when we go astray. *Preach it.*

- Confessional storytelling needs to become embedded in the church to change our DNA. You have your fingers on the pulse of stories which could/should be told. Everyone can benefit from the collateral blessing of transparency if you encourage others to share. Those stories could make a powerful difference in your church. *Show it.*

CHRIST-FOLLOWERS:

- God gave you a life story that has the ability to bless others, but this can only happen when you reveal your true self. Muster up the humility and courage to share with others how

God is transforming you. Don't squander your story, because there is collateral blessing meant for others buried in your mess. *Share it.*

• Encourage other followers of Christ to come out of hiding, and be patient and loving as they do. Remember, healing occurs when confession meets prayer, and you represent Christ's message of forgiveness. *Promote it.*

• God has good works planned just for you that take into consideration everything that makes up your life story. There are no accidents in this story. Sit down with other believers to consider what those good works might be. *Work it.*

• We need to see our pastors and leaders as humans who struggle with their fleshly desires. Yes, pastors will be held to a higher standard by God in His judgment, but that's His job. Everyone needs confession and forgiveness. *Give grace.*

• Church leaders get so little positive feedback in their work as shepherds. Go out of your way to encourage and bless your leaders. *Give blessings.*

• Be a sheep. Allow yourself to be led. Stay on the path. *Honor God with obedience.*

PUTTING A FACE ON CHRIST

Jesus Christ set an example for us in so many ways: love, humility, purity, diligence, and obedience to name a few. All of these run counter to our culture today, but Christ's humility stands out to me. The most striking facet of that part of Jesus's character is He embodied humility, and yet He's God! While here on Earth, Christ deserved all the glory He could have been given, but He demanded none.

God calls us to be ambassadors while we are alive, and that's a call to reflect Christ. As poor of a reflection as we might be, we also might be the only light someone else may need to visualize Christ. *So how could we put a face on Christ's humility here on Earth?*

- We can live transparent lives of humble confession.
- We can bear the shame of our disobedience without defensiveness.
- We can ask others for forgiveness when we have offended.
- We can offer forgiveness when we feel offended.
- We can show love to others when we don't feel they deserve it.

What if the world saw followers of Christ obeying the words of Paul from the book of Philippians: "Don't be selfish; don't try to impress others. Be humble, thinking of others as better than yourselves." (Philippians 2:3 NLT). That's how the world could see Christ reflected in us.

GOD CALLS US TO BE AMBASSADORS WHILE WE ARE ALIVE, AND THAT'S A CALL TO REFLECT CHRIST.

God's plan to show the world His message of forgiveness and reconciliation includes our willingness to openly share our struggles with others. We have a message to share both inside as well as outside the doors of our churches. Are you wasting your ability to deliver the message of God's love and forgiveness because you are afraid of others? Yes, we can be ambassadors of Christ, but we can't be that when we're hiding. Don't waste your message. God allowed so much to happen in your life that others need to hear.

Jesus Christ lived a life of humility, and we can give testimony to that part of Christ's nature through our humble, confessional storytelling. When we offer up our messy story, we live out our true selves, not some well-crafted, "Facebook worthy" false self. What would Facebook look like if everyone represented themselves with truth and transparency?

REFLECT GOD'S LIGHT

Christ-followers aren't called to hide their brokenness. We are called to transparency. The foundation of God's plan to free us from our guilt and shame lies in confession. We are also called to good works which God crafted for each of us. God did that so we might partner with Him to light the way for others to come to Christ.

> But you are a chosen people, royal priests, a holy nation, a people for God's own possession. You were chosen to tell about the wonderful acts of God, who called you out of darkness into his wonderful light. At one time you were not a people, but now you are God's people. In the past you had never received mercy, but now you have received God's mercy.
>
> Dear friends, you are like foreigners and strangers in this world. I beg you to avoid the evil things your bodies want to do that fight against your soul. People who do not believe are living all around you and might say that you are doing wrong. Live such good lives that they will see the good things you do and will give glory to God on the day when Christ comes again" (1 Peter 2:9-12 NCV).

If I could paraphrase Peter: *God chose you. He calls you out of darkness into the light so you can tell of His wonderful acts. God hates your secret place and the sin you want to keep secret. Push those actions away and live in God's mercy and grace. Your life is a testimony either for or against God. Make your life a righteous testimony bringing glory to God. He is worthy of the offering of your confessional story.*

Christ followers are Christ reflectors. Our good works reflect humility and gratitude for our forgiveness and salvation.

Are you offering your living testimony for others to see and hear? If not, when will you start?

FREEDOM

ARE YOU OFFERING YOUR LIVING TESTIMONY FOR OTHERS TO SEE AND HEAR? IF NOT, WHEN WILL YOU START?

The world longs for the message of Christ's redemption. Hiding prevents us from finding freedom and can muffle our ability to speak on behalf of our Savior. We find freedom through confession, repentance, and accountability, but what does that freedom mean?

Tim Chester sums up freedom in Christ so well: "Freedom is found in the truth that we were made to worship God, to serve God, to trust God. Freedom is found in acknowledging that we are responsible for the mess we have made of our lives, that our problems are rooted in our hearts, that we deserve God's judgment, that we desperately need God. Freedom is found in accepting that God is in control of our lives, that He is gracious, that He forgives those who come to Him in faith."[36]

Our guilt and shame-ridden world must hear this message. Lost souls who have been found, who have returned, have great reason to celebrate. Those people provide a powerful testimony for the community to see our God and our Savior, Jesus Christ, face-to-face.

God plans for each of us to do many good works, and *all of them happen outside of our hiding places.* As King David testified, forgiveness leads to great joy, and the lost hear shouts of deliverance. Sharing that joy and freedom with the world honors God and makes Him smile.

No one needs to be alone.

No one has to stay in hiding.

Those who allow God's light into their hiding place find freedom.

God is honored when freed people share His story of forgiveness, mercy, and grace.

FOR DISCUSSION

1. Paul wrote in Ephesians that you are God's masterpiece. (Ephesians 2:10) God gave you a specific story, crafted just for you, but that story is designed to give glory to God. (Isaiah 43:7) Are you sharing or wasting your message about God's glory through your life's story?

_____

_____

_____

_____

_____

_____

2. Sharing your story with others will require humility on your part. Philippians 2:3 tells us that we are to count others as more significant than ourselves. Our humble testimony may be the only way others see Christ in this world. Share why your pride may be holding you back from sharing.

_____

_____

_____

_____

_____

_____

3. Peter, Moses, David, and the Woman at the Well became a collateral blessing to many people. We know from reading 2 Timothy 2:21 we are to be set aside as holy and useful. Psalm 66:18-20 tells us that cherishing sin will prevent our prayers from being heard. Please pray for yourself and others in your group to step into God's good work through repentance.

_____

_____

_____

_____

_____

_____

4. If you are a follower of Christ, you are a new creation who has been chosen to be one of His voices. (1 Peter 2:9) Who do you know who needs to hear your voice tell of God's good work in your life?

_____

_____

_____

_____

_____

5. God brought you here to this very time in your life, and this is no accident. Nothing in your life ever was an accident. Because of your story, you are "uniquely suited" for a time such as this. I'm excited to hear where your path leads. Please share that path with me and with others.[37]

_____

_____

_____

_____

_____

_____

Endnotes

Introduction
1. Tim Chester. *You Can Change* (Wheaton: Crossway Books, 2010), 160.

Chapter 1: Grace and Mercy
2. Dietrich Bonhoeffer, *The Cost of Discipleship* (New York: Touchstone, 1995), 73.
3. Elyse Fitzpatrick, *Idols of the Heart* (Phillipsburg: P&R Publishing, 2001), 80.

Chapter 2: Distorted Worship
4. C.S. Lewis. *Mere Christianity* (New York: Collier, 1952), 109.
5. Paul David Tripp, *Instruments in the Redeemers Hands* (Phillipsburg: P&R Publishing, 2002) 71.
6. Tim Chester. *You Can Change* (Wheaton: Crossway Books, 2010), 123.

Chapter 3: True Worship
7. Kris Lundgaard, *The Enemy Within* (Phillipsburg: P&R Publishing, 1998), 101.

Chapter 4: Hiding
8. Rick Warren, The *Purpose Driven Life* (Grand Rapids: Zondervan, 2002), 213.
9. Edward Welch, *Addictions, A Banquet in the Grave* (Phillipsburg: P&R Publishing, 2001), 40.
10. Stephen Pattison, *Shame*: Theory, Therapy, Theology (Cambridge, U.K.:Cambridge University Press, 2000), 44.
11. Edward Welch, *Shame Interrupted* (Greensboro: New Growth Press, 2012), 280.
12. Dietrich Bonhoeffer, *Life Together* (Minneapolis: Fortress Press, 2015), 89.
13. John Bevere, *The Bait of Satan* (Lake Mary: Charisma House, 1997), 57.

CHAPTER 4: HIDING

14. Jay E. Adams, *A Theology of Christian Counseling* (Grand Rapids: Zondervan, 1979), 104.

15. John MacArthur, *The MacArthur Study Bible*-ESV (Wheaton: Crossway, 2010), Commentary-Romans 8:13, 1663

16. Elyse Fitzpatrick, *Idols of the Heart* (Phillipsburg: P&R Publishing, 2001), 177

17. John Baker, Life's Healing Choices (New York: Howard Books, 2017), 155.

18. Dietrich Bonhoeffer, *Life Together* (Minneapolis: Fortress Press, 2015), 88.

19. Elyse Fitzpatrick, *Idols of the Heart* (Phillipsburg: P&R Publishing, 2001), 146.

20. John Baker, *Life's Healing Choices* (New York: Howard Books, 2017), 157.

CHAPTER 6: REFUGE

21. Timothy Keller, *The Prodigal God* (New York:Penguin Books, 2011), 27-28.

CHAPTER 7: WE HAD TO CELEBRATE

22. Dietrich Bonhoeffer, *Life Together* (Minneapolis: Fortress Press, 2015), 87.

23. Max Lucado, Twitter post, Jan. 17, 2011.

CHAPTER 8: JOY IN FORGIVENESS

24. John MacArthur, *The Freedom and Power of Forgiveness* (Wheaton: Crossway Books, 1998), 161.

CHAPTER 9: CONFESSIONAL STORYTELLING

25. Michael Cheshire, *Why We Eat Our Own* (Denver: First Punch Press, 2013), 93.

26. Dietrich Bonhoeffer, *Life Together* (Minneapolis: Fortress Press, 2015), 92.

27. Edward Welch, *Addictions, A Banquet in the Grave* (Phillipsburg: P&R Publishing, 2001), 247.

28. Jerry Bridges, *Trusting God* (Colorado Springs: NavPress, 1988), 170.

29. https://churchleaders.com/pastors/pastor-articles/138266-pastors-sin-confession-and-the-catholics.html/4

30. https://www.christianitytoday.com/pastors/2012/summer/confession-max-lucado.html

CHAPTER 10: REPURPOSED

31. Dietrich Bonhoeffer, *Life Together* (Minneapolis: Fortress Press, 2015), 88-89.

32. John Piper, *Don't Waste Your Life* (Wheaton: Crossway, 2003), 65.

33. C.S. Lewis. *Mere Christianity* (New York: Collier, 1952), 176.

34. Dennis Rainey, *Choosing a Life That Matters* (Bloomington: Bethany House Publishers, 2017), 118.

35. Rick Warren, *The Purpose Driven Life* (Grand Rapids: Zondervan, 2002), 292.

36. Tim Chester. *You Can Change*, Wheaton: Crossway, 2010), 77.

Appendix

Distorted Worship Scriptures

EVERYONE IS GUILTY of a distortion of worship because the sins of Adam and Eve caused all of humanity to "fall" away from God. In this appendix, you will find numerous Bible verses that address some of the most common worship distortions.

In the list below, you will find actions which should be "put off" and what actions need to be "put on" to pursue sanctification. Because all sin stems from a prideful heart that desires its own way, it should come as no surprise that humility is the underlying solution to so many issues of life. Please excuse the resulting redundancy in the solutions offered. That redundancy can be traced to two Scriptures, which, if followed, would eliminate so many issues in our lives:

> And He said to him, "You shall love the Lord your God with all your heart and with all your soul and with all your mind. This is the great and first commandment. And a second is like it: You shall love your neighbor as yourself. On these two commandments depend all the Law and the Prophets" (Matthew 22:37-40).

> Do nothing from selfish ambition or conceit, but in humility count others more significant than yourselves (Philippians 2:3).

Anger: Anger stems from a self-focused heart that places one's own desires above God and others. Refocusing on first understanding God's desires and the needs and desires of others is how anger can be resolved.

Anxiety and Fear: Anxiety and fear are the result of a prideful heart looking to control and resolve problems without relying on God. Trusting in God for His provision and care pushes away anxiety and fear.

Envy: Envying, jealousy and coveting go hand-in-hand because a prideful heart can never be satisfied. It will always desire more. Envy is closely related to anger because the focus is on self, and not on God's provision or the needs of others.

Gluttony: Gluttony and its cousin, drunkenness place their focus on self-comfort found in food and drink. The lives of gluttons and drunkards are less concerned about serving God and others with a healthy lifestyle than they are with attempts to satisfy personal gratification.

Greed: Greedy people store up treasure for themselves. Instead of serving God and others with the assets which God provided, they hold onto those blessings as if God was incapable of blessing them with even more. Greed is cured by cultivating a heart for serving God and others with the assets God has allowed one to manage.

Judgmentalism: Judgmentalism straddles Pride and Anger. A prideful heart will look to judge others in order to feel better about oneself. This can also result in an angry outcome because the prideful heart assumes it knows what's best for everyone. Understanding that God has gifted everyone differently and specifically helps rein in a judgmental heart.

Lust: Lust seeks to fulfill its own fleshly desires above God's desires or the well-being of others. Serving God and the good of others requires the self-control of reining in inappropriate passions.

Pride: By now it should be evident that humility is the cure for pride. This isn't thinking less of oneself, it's thinking about oneself less. Again, this requires placing a focus on serving God and others.

Sins of the Tongue: Like Judgmentalism, Sins of the Tongue make a prideful heart feel better about oneself. These are hostile ways that humans treat others (and God) with inappropriate words. God gave man a tongue to lift Him and others up, not to tear down.

Sloth: Sloth isn't a term used much anymore, but it relates to laziness. A heart that is lazy and slothful concerns itself with self-comfort, ease and relaxation. The self-sacrifice of putting God's agenda and the needs of others above self helps to avoid laziness and sloth.

Ungodliness: Ungodliness falls last in this list, but is the summation of all other worship distortions. If human hearts placed God on the throne where He belongs, there would be no ungodliness, or any of the other issues above.

In addition to God's Word, I appreciate two resources in developing this Appendix:

Jerry Bridges, *Respectable Sins* (Colorado Springs: NavPress, 2007).

https://www.bibleinfo.com/en/questions/what-are-seven-deadly-sins

Bible verses that address some of the most common worship distortions	
Adultery	See: Lust Exodus 20:14 Proverbs 6:32 Matthew 5:27-32
Anger	Psalm 37:8 Proverbs 14:29 Proverbs 15:1

Anxiety/Fear	Romans 12:19 Ephesians 4:26-27 Colossians 3:8 James 1:19-20 Matthew 6:25-34 Matthew 10:31 Mark 9:24 Luke 12:7 Philippians 4:6 1 Peter 5:7
Arrogance	See: Pride
Bitterness	See: Anger, Judgmentalism
Boastful	See: Pride
Competitiveness	See: Pride
Coveting	See: Envy, Lust
Critical spirit	See: Judgmentalism
Debauchery	See: Gluttony, Lust
Deceit	See: Sins of the Tongue
Depravity	See: Lust
Desire for Comfort	See: Sloth
Discontentment	See: Anger
Discord	See: Anger, Sins of the Tongue

Dishonoring Parents	See: Pride
Dissensions	See: Anger
Doctrinal Judgmentalism	See: Judgmentalism, Pride
Drunkenness	See: Gluttony
Enmity	See: Anger, Sins of the Tongue

Envy

Exodus 20:1-17
Job 5:2
Psalm 37:1
Proverbs 14:30
Proverbs 24:19-20
Ecclesiastes 4:4
Galatians 5:26
James 3:14-16

Evil	See: Ungodliness
Faction	See: Pride
False Worship	See: Pride, Ungodliness
Fear	See: Anxiety/Fear
Frustration	See: Anger, Anxiety/Fear

Gluttony

Psalm 78:17-19
Proverbs 23:1-3
Proverbs 23:19-21
1 Corinthians 3:16-17
1 Corinthians 10:31
Galatians 5
Philippians 3:19-20

God-haters	See: Pride, Ungodliness
Gossip	See: Envy, Pride, Sins of the Tongue
Greed	Exodus 20:17 Proverbs 11:24 Proverbs 28:25 Ecclesiastes 5:10 Philippians 4:6 1 Timothy 6:9-10 Hebrews 13:5
Grudge	See: Anger, Envy, Judgmentalism
Hatred	See: Anger
Hostility	See: Anger, Sins of the Tongue
Idolatry	See: Pride, Ungodliness
Impatience	See: Anger
Impurity	See: Lust, Ungodliness
Independent Spirit	See: Pride
Invent ways of Doing Evil	See: Ungodliness
Irritability	See: Anger
Jealousy	See: Envy
Judgementalism	Matthew 7:1-5 Romans 14:4

Lack of Self-Control	See: Gluttony
Laziness	See: Sloth
Life of Ease	See: Sloth
Lust	Exodus 20:1-17 Job 31:1 Matthew 5:27-32 Philippians 4:8 2 Timothy 2:22 James 1:14-15 1 Peter 2:11 1 John 2:16
Lying/Libel	See: Sins of the Tongue
Malice	See: Anger
Misusing God's Name	See: Ungodliness
Murder	See: Anger
Orgies	See: Lust
Pride **Pride (cont.)**	Proverbs 8:13 Proverbs 16:18 Jeremiah 9:23-24 Romans 1 Romans 12:16 1 Corinthians 13:4 2 Corinthians 12:20-21 Galatians 6:3 James 4:6-7

Pride of Achievement	See: Pride
Pride of Moral Self-Righteousness	See: Pride
Pursuit of relaxation	See: Sloth
Resentment	See: Anger, Greed
Selfish Ambition	See: Greed, Pride
Selfishness	See: Greed, Pride
Sexual Immorality	See: Lust
Sins of the Tongue	Exodus 20:1-17 Psalm 19:14 Matthew 12:34-36 Romans 1 2 Corinthians 12:20-21 Galatians 5 Ephesians 4:29 James 3
Slander	Sins of the Tongue
Sloth	Proverbs 6:6 Proverbs 13:4 Proverbs 24:33-34
Sloth (Cont.)	Romans 12:11-13 Colossians 3:23 2 Thessalonians 3:10
Sluggard	See: Sloth

Stealing	See: Envy. Greed
Strife	See: Anger
Unforgiving	See: Anger
Ungodliness	Exodus 20:1-17 Romans 1 Galatians 5
Violating the Sabbath	See: Ungodliness
Wickedness	See: Lust
Witchcraft	See: Ungodliness
Worldliness	See: Lust
Worry	See: Anxiety/Fear

ACKNOWLEDGMENTS

"When I sit down to write a book, I do not say to myself, 'I am going to produce a work of art.' I write it because there is some lie that I want to expose, some fact to which I want to draw attention, and my initial concern is to get a hearing."

George Orwell

I SAT DOWN to write *Why We Hide* because of the lies of one being, Satan. He's known by so many names, but "Satan the Liar" should be close to the top of that list. *Why We Hide* exists to expose the lies Satan whispers to all of us every day.

Through these pages I hope you hear the truth found in God's Word about who you are in God's eyes. He has a great love for you. His desire is that you live in the security of that fact so you pursue all the good works He has planned for you.

Many people offered invaluable insight in birthing *Why We Hide*. I especially owe a huge debt of gratitude to two friends with decades of editing experience: Georgia Varozza and Paul Danison. I appreciate the art and craft behind Georgia's detailed oversight. Paul brought the cut-throat view of a newspaper editor who often asked: "So What?" and "Who Cares?"

In addition, many others offered their discerning questions and comments. In alphabetical order, they are: April Brandes, Chris Brynzeel, Conny Crisalli, Diane Diggs, Iris Durfee, Lindsay Gann, Ryan Gauss, Andrew Hartman, Kelly Hartman, Ruth Hartman, Steve Larson, Connie Larson, Keith Mathias, John Schoolland, Dwayne Strivens, Lora Van Dixhorn and Rita Warren. All of you helped in making *Why We Hide* a more mature and worthwhile effort.

Made in the USA
Columbia, SC
02 September 2021